D0859812

RAISING
THE
STANDARD

RAISING
THE
STANDARD

CARMAN
WITH
WALTER WALKER

Sparrow Press
Nashville, Tennessee

© 1994 Carman Licciardello

All rights reserved. Written permission must be secured from the publisher to use or reproduce any part of this book, except for brief quotations in critical reviews or articles.

Published 1994 in Nashville, Tennessee, by
Sparrow Press
101 Winners Circle
Brentwood, TN 37024-5010
Distributed in Canada by Christian Marketing Canada, Ltd.

Printed in the United States of America

98 97 96 95 94   5 4 3 2 1

Library of Congress Cataloging-in-Publication Data

Carman, 1956-
      Raising the standard: reclaiming our world for God / Carman with Walter Walker.
         p.   cm.
      ISBN 0-917143-33-7 : $14.95
        1. Christianity—United States—20th Century—Miscellanea.
2. Carman, 1956-   —Interviews. I. Walker, Walter, 1953-
II. Title.
BR526.C375 1994
248.4—dc20   93-46226
                                       CIP

Quotations and song lyrics in each chapter are from the following:

Ch. 1 "America Again" by Carman & Michael Omartian © 1993 Some-O-Dat Music (Administered by WORD INC.)/Middle C Music and Edward Grant, Inc. (Administered by Reunion Music) All Rights Reserved. Used by Permission.
"Marchin' and Movin'" by Carman & Gary Oliver © 1993 Some-O-Dat Music/CMI-HP Publishing (Both administered by WORD INC.) All Rights Reserved. Used By Permission.
Ch. 3 "America Again" by Carman & Michael Omartian.
Ch. 7 "Aquarius" © 1966, 1967, 1968, 1970 James Rado, Gerome Ragni, Galt MacDermot, Nat Shapiro, c/o EMI U Catalog Inc. Used by permission of CPP Belwin. Inc., Miami, FL. A.R.R. I.C.S.
Ch. 8 "He Looked Beyond My Faults" by Dottie Rambo © 1968 John T. Benson Publishing Co. All Rights Reserved. Used by permission of Benson Music Group, Inc.
Ch. 9 "Nothing But The Blood Of Jesus" (Public Domain).

All Scripture quotations, unless otherwise noted, are from the Holy Bible, New International Version. © 1973, 1978, 1984 International Bible Society. Used by permission of Zondervan Bible Publishers.
Scripture quotations noted KJV are from the King James Version of the Bible.
Quotations noted Williams are from the *New Testament: A Private Translation in the Language of the People,* by Charles B. Williams, Moody Press, Chicago, 1963.

Jacket design by Joyce Revoir.
Book design by Mike Goodson.

CONTENTS

ACKNOWLEDGMENTS

Special thanks to

Laura Arant for her painstaking research on the book.

Dr. Mark Rutland for his help with the material on *The Devil Goes Too Far.*

Bill Hoesch of the Institute for Creation Research for his critique of chapter 5.

My family, friends, and staff for their prayers, constant support, and involvment with this book and the ministry.

Bill Hearn and the staff at Sparrow for joining with me as we "Raise the Standard."

Finally, to my Lord Jesus Christ who set the ultimate "standard" for us all.

FOREWORD

Carman, in his new book *Raising the Standard,* calls this nation back to its Christian foundations. A good idea—or is it? After all, are there any Christian foundations left to go back to? Or, more important, were there ever any?

Yes, America began upon Christian foundations, according to many Founding Fathers, early Congresses and Supreme Courts:

- *The general principles on which the fathers achieved independence were . . . the general principles of Christianity . . . Now I will avow that I then believed, and now believe, that those general principles of Christianity are as eternal and immutable as the existence and attributes of God.* (JOHN ADAMS, U.S. PRESIDENT)

- *The rights essential to happiness . . . we claim . . . from the King of Kings, and Lord of all the earth.* (JOHN DICKINSON, SIGNER OF THE U.S. CONSTITUTION)

- *Let us enter [the American Revolution] under the idea that we are Christians on whom the eyes of the world are now turned . . . Let us . . . humbly and penitently implore the Aid of the Almighty God, whom we profess to serve—let us earnestly call and beseech him for Christ's sake to preside in our councils.* (ELIAS BOUDINOT, PRESIDENT OF CONGRESS DURING THE AMERICAN REVOLUTION)

- *The Declaration of Independence first organized the social compact on the foundation of the Redeemer's mission upon the earth [and] laid the corner stone of human government upon the first precepts of Christianity.* (JOHN QUINCY ADAMS, U.S. PRESIDENT)

- *The wise and great men of those days were not ashamed publicly to confess the name of our blessed Lord and Savior Jesus Christ! in behalf of the people, as their representatives and rulers, they acknowledged the sublime doctrine of his mediation!* (RICHARD HENRY LEE, 1825, GRANDSON OF THE SIGNER OF THE U.S. DECLARATION OF INDEPENDENCE)

- *We are a Christian people.* (U.S. SENATE, 1853, U.S. SUPREME COURT, 1931)

- *Christianity . . . was the religion of the founders of the republic, and they expected it to remain the religion of their descendents.* (U.S. HOUSE OF REPRESENTATIVES, 1854)

- *This is a Christian nation.* (U.S. SUPREME COURT, 1892)

Despite our auspicious beginnings, raising the standard of Christianity again today seems an impossible task, judging by the noise level of the opposition. But Carman is absolutely right when he says, "The enemies of righteousness and the opponents of Christianity are not nearly as powerful as they appear."

Interestingly, the biggest obstacle to raising the standard again is not "them," it's "us." so what should we do? As Carman explains, "Jump out of the foxhole, pick up the standard, and courageously lead the way."

Indeed, "why sit we here till we die" (2 Kings 7:3), for we have a "great cloud of witnesses" (Heb. 12:1) watching us to see what we will do; and *they* know we can do it, but do *we?* Are we really strong enough for the task? That same question was asked by our own Founding Fathers long ago and was answered by Patrick Henry:

> *They tell us, sir, that we are weak—unable to cope with so formidable an adversary. But when shall we be stronger? Will it be next week, or next year? . . . Shall we gather strength by irresolution and inaction? . . . Sir, we are not weak if we make a proper use of those means which the God of nature hath placed in our power.*

This is still our answer today—rely on God and get busy! In this book, Carman shows us the attitudes to develop and the steps we can take to help raise the standard again.

David Barton

"It will be good for that servant whom the master finds *doing* so when he returns." (Jesus, Luke 12:43)

THE ENEMY'S COMING LIKE A FLOOD

(But the Lord Is Raising a Standard)

Imagine you are

. . . a student in a rural village school early in the last century. You've worked hard all morning, studying the great philosophers so that you can learn how to distinguish good thought from weak thought, right from wrong. Now you're practicing penmanship by copying some important character-building truths from an old English volume, proud to think that these are the same traits on which kings and statesmen like George Washington built their lives. You write, "When you speak of God or his attributes, let it be seriously, in reverence and honor, and obey your natural parents."[1]

When you stand and move toward the front of the classroom to lay your paper on the instructor's desk, however, something incomprehensible happens. Unknowingly, you've walked through the beam of a time-probe that propels you through time to the twentieth century . . .

And suddenly, you find yourself in a strange classroom, full of people your age who have pierced various places on their head with unusual metal objects. While your mouth is hanging open, the teacher grabs your paper and reads your statement. When she sees the word *God*, she gets pale. "Look," she says, "I think you'd better head for the principal's office. We don't allow this kind of stuff in our schools. You can't force your narrow, bigoted, religious thoughts on the rest of us . . . And while you're at it, lose the weird threads."

Okay, so it sounds funny when you put it like that. But our situation isn't really funny anymore. Something is seriously wrong in our world. We Christians have been busy with Bible studies, conferences and building strong churches—and every bit of that is good. We need strong churches, like modern-day arks, to carry us through the flood-tide that's coming. But even though I see storm clouds rising and smell rain in the air, I haven't heard God tell me to run and hide yet. In fact, when I pray, I hear God telling me the opposite.

Could They Bust You for Being a Christian?

"What's next, Lord?" That's the question I had asked God over and over. "Lord, show me what's in your heart. What's our next direction?"

The Lord told us to be *radically saved,* to get *addicted to Jesus* and believe for *revival in the land.* Many good ideas were suggested, and we could have followed any one of them. But I've learned my lesson: Good ideas are not enough. Real success requires seeking God's heart and God's purpose. Jesus said that if you seek, you'll find, if you search with all your heart. After months of listening to God, it became clear. These *radically saved, addicted-to-Jesus* Christians who are praying for *revival in the land* are to do something more. They are to raise a standard and re-take our world for God. The front lines of our battle are all too clear. In America, for instance, something has happened since Thomas Jefferson called the Bible the cornerstone.

> *Something happened since Jefferson called the Bible*
>   *the cornerstone,*
> *For American liberty then put it in our schools as a*
>   *light.*
> *Or since "Give me liberty or give me death," Patrick*
>   *Henry said,*
> *Our country was founded upon the gospel of Jesus*
>   *Christ.*
> *We eliminated God from the equation of American life,*
> *Thus eliminating the reason this nation first began.*
> *From beyond the grave I hear the voices of our*
>   *founding fathers plead,*
> *"You need God in America again."*

("America Again" by Carman and
Michael Omartian)

It is becoming increasingly difficult to live as a Christian in what some call the "post-Christian era." What's happening? It's as if we woke up one day, and someone changed all the rules. It seems like the restraining walls that held back a flood of evil have been breached, and we're drowning in the rising tide of filth and corruption. Things that were completely unthinkable within the last decade are now cool and acceptable. A few years ago no one would have believed the kind of moral and social issues we are debating today. Those who stand for what is right are ridiculed and discounted, while enemies of righteousness are protected and promoted.

> *In the '40s and '50s student problems were chewing*
> *   gum and talking.*
> *In the '90s, rape and murder are the trend.*
> *The only way this nation can even hope to last this*
> *   decade*
> *Is to put God in America again.*

("America Again")

Not only are moral standards disappearing, but the freedoms to live, believe and speak as a Christian are being lost one by one. When students are bold enough to take a stand for Christ on high school campuses by praying, witnessing or having a Bible study, they find that it's forbidden.

They are told by authorities, "You can't do that sort of thing here."

I think it is time for something to be done. It's time for every blood-bought, born-again Christian to stand up, be counted as a disciple of Jesus Christ and begin recovering what we have allowed the powers of darkness to steal. It's time to raise the standard of Christianity over our world again.

As Christians in a free Western culture we have a great responsibility. Religious liberty and righteous government are precious gifts passed to us by the grace of God and the sacrifice of many. I don't want to be a part of a generation responsible for carelessly losing it all without first taking a stand. I want to be a part of the generation that experiences a nationwide spiritual awakening and renewing of righteousness throughout the land.

From Christian leaders to newscasters, everyone is telling us how bad things are. Unfortunately, it's true, and I'll point out some of our difficulties in the following chapters. But my reason for writing this book is simply this: I am convinced that the Spirit who empowers us is greater than the spirit who empowers all the forces that come against the standards of God. Therefore, I believe that there are three truths God wants this generation to stand on:

- First, the enemies of righteousness and the opponents of Christianity are not nearly as powerful as they appear, so we should not give in to fear or discouragement (Josh. 1:9).
- Second, taking a bold stand for Christ has more effect than we realize on both the spiritual and physical world around us (Eph. 3:8-12).
- Third, we may be the key to revival in this generation and the return to a strong, living Christianity as the standard in our society.

Revivals and spiritual awakenings don't happen by themselves. God uses people who he has helped break free from the intimidation of the darkness and spiritual deadness of their surroundings. An evidence of being filled with the Holy Spirit is that we speak the truth with boldness and confidence, no matter what the consequences.

In 1986, Steve Hall started a Bible study in a fraternity house at the University of Arizona. Eventually Ian Laks, the president of the fraternity, gave his life to Christ. Eleven months later, Brian Smith became a Christian as well. Both began to take a bold stand for Jesus Christ everywhere they went. Brian was elected president of the Intrafraternity Council the following year. One Bible study spawned another. Eight years later, as a direct result of that one Bible study, there are seventy evangelistic Bible studies and fifty Christian discipleship groups held every week on the campus of the University of Arizona. Three student senators attend. One of them, Trent Grimet, is one of the most radically saved, bold witnesses for Christ on campus.

In the Fall semester of 1993, over thirty students gave their lives to Christ as a result of those Bible studies. Twenty-three of them were baptized as well.

This spiritual turn-around won't come to our campuses and communities without faith, prayer, courage and commitment. But it's that kind of bold Christianity that's exciting and victorious. We have been hiding in the shadows too long. We are soldiers of the cross, and it is time to start marching.

We're marchin' and movin' onward and upward.
The kingdom of God is on a forceful advance.

We are takin' dominion over the darkness,
Tearin' down the works of the enemy's hands.

("Marchin' and Movin'," by Carman and
Gary Oliver)

Marching and Moving

Some of the world's most spectacular events have taken place on battlefields where great armies of history met. Huge forces—on some occasions over a hundred thousand uniformed soldiers—have stretched across the plains as far as the eye can see. Such great hosts are always organized into companies, regiments and battalions, each unit with its own commander and each with its own flag or banner. Once a battle begins, order and ceremony turn to chaos and confusion. Troops sometimes are scattered, cut off from their units or simply lost and disoriented. In the mayhem, soldiers separated from their units don't know if they are about to be overrun and captured by the enemy or left behind by the advancement of their comrades. Being lost, alone and confused on a battlefield is terrifying.

The flags and banners of an army are called *standards*. Historically, one of the most important and most honored duties a soldier could be given is carrying the flag. These banners and flags were not merely for decoration. They represented the pride and purpose of the army, and served a strategic purpose. The troops stayed in their ranks and knew which way to go by following the standard-bearer.

Imagine how important it was to an enemy to capture or

destroy your standard. Your whole army would be thrown into confusion. So, if ever the standard-bearer fell, it became the responsibility of the closest soldier to him to pick up the flag and continue the advance. "Never let the colors touch the ground" was the standing order.

Dropping a rifle to pick up a flag doesn't make a lot of sense at first. But when you realize the function of keeping a standard held high, it becomes more important than carrying a weapon. Without it the troops will be scattered and confused. The flag or the standard is the rallying point.

Comin' Like a Flood

Throughout our world today, Christians seem confused, disoriented and afraid. For many believers, it's like looking out over the edge of a foxhole and seeing a horizon cluttered with an assortment of banners boldly lifted high by the enemies of righteousness.

Militant homosexuals, pro-abortionists, occultists, New Agers, pornographers, radical feminists, atheists, paganists and a whole collection of angry anti-Christian groups are all coming out of their closets and onto the battlefield. Their common denominator is a hatred for Christianity and for any expression of traditional values.

That's not an encouraging sight. We seem to be surrounded by people with their guns loaded, just waiting for someone to take a stand for righteousness. The natural inclination is to stay in the hole and keep your head down. That's where many Christians are—intimidated, afraid and laying low.

The truth is, there's nothing new about any of these groups or their anti-Christian sentiments. They've been around for years. But something has happened in the last few years that has given them a new boldness and a new confidence.

Over the last ten years in America, for example, the American Civil Liberties Union (ACLU) has actively pursued people who will bring suit against almost every public expression of Christianity. The National Organization for Women (NOW) and other radical feminist organizations seem to oppose all traditional Christian values. Their battle cry is "We're here, we're feminist and we're in your face." Though a small minority, they have become powerful by setting themselves up as the representative voice on all women's issues.

Militant homosexual groups such as Act Up are out of the closet and boldly promoting a debased social agenda. On April 25, 1993, a march for homosexual rights took place in Washington, D.C. A video of the march produced by Christian Action Network showed footage of self-identified members of leather fetish communities, a man demonstrating how to use a condom on a sex toy, and a group called Church Ladies for Choice, singing *God Is a Lesbian* to the tune of *My Country Tis of Thee.*[2]

Alyson Press of Boston, the leading producer of homosexual literature, recently published *Gay Sex: A Manual for Men Who Love Boys.* This and one of Alyson's earlier publications, *The Age Taboo: Gay Male Sexuality, Power and Consent*, are written for child molesters and would-be molesters.[3]

Thousands of witches gather each year in Salem,

Massachusetts, to learn from each other and to encourage each other to be bolder about their occultic practices.

In recent years, these groups have become powerfully entrenched. While the righteous seed in America abandoned their watch, the enemy has come in like a flood.

As a result, in many places—at our workplaces, on our campuses or in our classrooms—we feel spiritual opposition to boldly proclaiming the truth. Why is it that enemies of righteousness now feel free to boldly proclaim their ideas and raise their standards high, while Christians feel opposition and intimidation? As Christians, we know that it's not a matter of what's "cool" and what's "in," but it is a matter of coming against spiritual principalities and powers.

The enemies of righteousness have always hidden in dark corners, afraid to come out into the light. When the standard of Christianity falls and the light of the gospel is diminished, then the dark feels at liberty to boldly assert itself. As a result, students are mocked and persecuted in schools. In the workplace and in government, Christianity is ridiculed. Why? In part because the mockers simply fill the vacuum left as the forces of the Kingdom of Light are scattered, feeling intimidated by the darkness.

If we think the answer is to hide from the dark, or to keep our mouths shut to avoid mocking, we'd better think again.

The 20/60/20 Rule

Intimidation often comes in the form of being excluded from the "in crowd." You don't have to go into some foreign territory to experience this. Even in a Christian school, a Christian college or your own church, you may be labeled as weird, uncool or fanatical if you take a stand and try to live a radically-saved lifestyle. What does it mean to be cool anyway? If it means being what other people want you to be, forget it. Being cool can mean that you're not cold, but you're not hot either. You're only average—lukewarm. Jesus said, **"So, because you are lukewarm—neither hot nor cold—I am about to spit you out of my mouth" (Rev. 3:16).**

A 20/60/20 rule applies to most groups. Usually, twenty percent are committed to one set of beliefs or lifestyle, and another twenty percent are committed to the opposite ideology or lifestyle. The rest of the people, the remaining sixty percent, simply lean in the direction of the twenty percent that's the boldest and most assertive. This sixty percent is made up of the followers—they usually don't speak with any strong personal convictions, they parrot what they hear the "in-crowd" say.

I believe many think that Christianity is uncool for two reasons: First, some small groups of people have become committed enemies of righteousness. Second, Christians have allowed themselves to be intimidated. As a result, the middle sixty percent has followed the lead of the unbelievers, thinking that irreverence and rebellion are good.

Let me tell you who I think is *cool*—those who know the God of the universe in a personal way through Jesus Christ, and who understand they have all power over the enemy. They live their lives according to the unalterable, unchangeable Word of God.

Their friends, classmates, co-workers and even the hosts of heaven and hell know that they are a greater threat to the evil of their day than evil is to them.

When a few Christians begin to take a bold stand—in classrooms and locker rooms, on the job and in private conversation, in youth groups and on the streets— they'll find others who have been waiting for someone to stop being a follower and to lead the way. There will be those who are so committed to their way of life they hear nothing we say. But most people are in the middle group, following what is currently popular. It doesn't take many Christians living all-out for God to make following Christ not just the cool thing to do, but the *only* thing to do. Every time a Christian takes a bold stand—every time we share the gospel or say no to those who want to intimidate us—we rediscover our strength in Christ. And we find that there are a lot of Christians in that middle sixty percent, lying low in their foxholes, who will climb out and join us in standing for the Lord as soon as the standard is raised. Why are we hesitating?

Out of That Closet!

I am committed to Christ, and not ashamed of him. I've determined in my life to fly the flag high. No one has to wonder what I'm about—they quickly realize I'm a disciple of Jesus Christ. Be honest—are you an undercover Christian? Are you hiding your light under a trash can of coolness? Jesus said to let your light shine on a hill so everyone can see it.

Every year homosexuals have a coming-out day. Men, women

and teenagers "come out of the closet" and proudly choose to live an openly perverted lifestyle. It's true that as Christians we're told to go into our closets to pray—but we're not told to live there! We don't need a coming-out day for Christians—we need a *charging-out day!* It's time we take a stand.

One of the most inspiring letters I have ever received came from a mother in Minnesota who, along with her husband, is raising her children to be standard-bearers for Christ. Here is a portion of that letter:

> *Dear Carman,*
>
> *My name is Sandy Miller. I am the mother of four children— three girls and one boy. The two oldest girls are teenagers. The youngest girl and our son are ages nine and seven. My husband, Kris, and I try very hard to raise our children to know the Lord personally, and in today's age that is not always easy. The reason I am writing to you is this:*
>
> *Today is the day set aside nationwide for "See You at the Pole," a chance for all high school students across the world to gather at their campus flagpoles to pray to the Lord for help in the school year. Our oldest daughter, Andrea, decided that this was something she really wanted to do. We supported her completely.*
>
> *She made some posters to hang up in her (public) school, but was told she could not put them up. She then decided to spread the word through church bulletins and by word of mouth. She spent much time in prayer*

and in preparing materials for the event. She planned to use Scriptures and songs as well as some of her own thoughts, and to encourage others to add their comments.

As the big day arrived she was up early, excited to be a witness of her faith. Though the night before brought our first frost, it did not dampen her spirits. I dropped the girls at school (we live in the country), and stayed awhile to see what would happen.

When the time came on that cold, foggy Minnesota morning for "See You at the Pole," the only ones standing beneath the flag praying and praising the Lord were Andrea, her sister, Kristina, age 14, and her sister, Miranda, age 9.

I have never loved my children more or been as proud of them as I was that morning. They continued praying and praising, even though other students smirked at them as they passed by. I sat in our van and prayed for them, thanking the Lord and asking that they would always know him as they knew him that morning. I could visualize him standing proudly beside them, holding their hearts in his hand. Sometimes the walk with Jesus can be very lonely.

It was not easy for them to stand there, especially when friends who had promised to join them did not show up. I saw the tears in their eyes as I told them they were not alone—the Lord had been there too.

I was moved by that letter. How about you? Are you willing to come out of the closet as a Christian and join bold young heroes of the faith like Andrea, Kristina and Miranda?

If I Be Lifted Up . . .

We in America are a lot like the children of Israel. They forgot how God miraculously delivered them from tyranny. After constant rebellion and disobedience, they found themselves under the judgment of God. Fiery serpents came in among the people and bit them. Many of them died.

> **The Lord said to Moses, "Make a snake and put it up on a pole; anyone who is bitten can look at it and live." So Moses made a bronze snake and put it up on a pole. Then when anyone was bitten by a snake and looked at the bronze snake, he lived. (Num. 21:8-9)**

We often find Christians with their heads down, not talking about Jesus Christ because they mistakenly believe that nobody wants to hear and nobody wants to be saved. That's the biggest lie ever dished out of Satan's kitchen. There are people all around you who have been "snake bitten" by sin and are feeling the effects of its venom. They are desperate for someone to show them that Christ is the answer. As Jesus said to Nicodemus:

> **Just as Moses lifted up the snake in the desert, so the Son of Man must be lifted up, that everyone who**

believes in him may have eternal life. For God so loved the world that he gave his one and only Son, that whoever believes in him shall not perish but have eternal life. (John 3:14-16)

The last thing the enemies of righteousness want to happen is for some Spirit-empowered Christian to come out of hiding, raise the standard of the gospel of Jesus Christ and bring light to a people who live in darkness. Satan's goal is to have the world follow him into greater and greater darkness. Misery loves company, you know. But if Christ is lifted up, Satan knows the world will follow him, and he will lose his place of power and influence. Satan will have to go back into the closet because the light of the gospel will reveal him.

Jesus said, " . . . Now is the time for judgment on this world; now the prince of this world will be driven out. But I, when I am lifted up from the earth, will draw all men to myself." (John 12:30-32)

Me—a Standard Bearer?

The movie *Glory* was based on the letters of Colonel Robert Gould Shaw, the commander of the first black regiment in the United States Army. The final scenes of the film recreated the heroic charge of Shaw's Massachusetts 54th regiment on Fort Wagner, the Confederate stronghold near Charleston, South Carolina.

Before the dawn assault, Colonel Shaw pointed to the regiment's standard-bearer and said to the men, "If this man should fall, who will lift the flag and carry it on?" Thomas Earl, the boyhood friend of Shaw and the one singled out by the drill sergeant as the weakest and worst soldier in the regiment, surprised everyone by boldly stepping forward. "*I* will!" he said.

That night the remnants of the Massachusetts 54th advanced to the perimeter of the garrison and were pinned down under heavy fire. Colonel Shaw, who led the charge out of the foxhole against the enemy line, was dead. Who would pick up the flag and lead the advance? It wasn't the strongest and most decorated soldiers. Nor was it the newly-bold Thomas Earl. Instead, it was a Private Tripp—a soldier who once had deserted his regiment—who raised the standard and led the troops on.

Perhaps you've been reading these challenging words and struggling with a sense of failure or unworthiness. But God can use the weakest person—he even uses those who once deserted! Because of his fear, John Mark left Paul and Barnabas when things became difficult and ran home to his mother in Jerusalem (Acts 13:13; 15:37-38). Later he became a valued associate of both Paul and Peter, wrote one of the gospels and, according to early church historians, became the founder and pastor of the church in Alexandria. Peter, the deserter who denied the Lord three times, became the great apostle of the early church and, eventually, the leader of the church in Rome.

No matter how incapable or weak you may feel, God has supernatural strength for you far beyond anything you have imagined. Like salvation, you can't earn it—you can only receive it by an act of faith. It doesn't matter how many times you've blown it, God still wants to use you.

Consider this: Fort Wagner was never taken by the Union regiment, but that one battle is not the point. Word spread of the bravery of the Massachusetts 54th. The stand made by a few men led Congress to finally approve recruitment of black troops throughout the Union, and approximately 180,000 volunteered. President Abraham Lincoln credited these regiments with turning the tide of the Civil War.

In the dark days of their sin, Isaiah prophesied to the nation of Israel of God's plan to raise up one to stand in the gap:

> **And he saw that there was no man, and wondered that there was no intercessor: therefore his arm brought salvation unto him; and his righteousness, it sustained him. For he put on righteousness as a breastplate, and an helmet of salvation upon his head; and he put on the garments of vengeance for clothing, and was clad with zeal as a cloak . . . So shall they fear the name of the Lord from the west, and his glory from the rising of the sun. *When the enemy shall come in like a flood, the Spirit of the Lord shall lift up a standard against him.* (Isaiah 59:16-17, 19, KJV)**

Our society, for the most part, is rushing headlong into hell. Who's the one—in your workplace, in your classroom or in your circle of friends—to take a stand for Christ in the midst of opposition? I believe that standard-bearer is you.

I believe you are called to come out of your closet and start flying the flag high as a fearless disciple of Jesus Christ. You are to be as bold in your personal world as I am in mine.

The question is, will you take a stand, along with me and many other Christians today?

In this book, I hope to help you find your place on the front lines of a battle that is coming soon to a town near you. Or maybe it's there already. I want to show you several important things:

•First, the battle-plan that I believe is God's word to us for this strategic hour in our history.

•Second, a look at what the opponents of our faith are up to as they push their anti-Christian agendas.

•Third, some true reports about other Christians who are boldly taking a stand, and recapturing their personal world for God.

•Fourth, some simple strategies that you can use as the front line of battle edges into your world.

Or maybe you feel like you're out on the front lines *now*—on your job, on your school campus or in your neighborhood. If that's so, then you need a word of encouragement before you read on. I believe we can win today's battle. Why do I say that?

Because we are blood-bought members of the most powerful army that ever walked the earth. We are filled with the same Spirit that raised Christ Jesus from the dead. We are to be champions.

Time 2
RAISE THE STANDARD

It's not unusual for Christians to find themselves pinned down, hiding in their favorite foxhole. They are grieved because they see false religions and the enemies of righteousness being exalted. They also are beginning to hear the voice of the Holy Spirit speaking to their heart, calling them to raise the standard.

If you are one of those lying low in a foxhole, what do you do? Here are some suggestions for setting a new direction for your life:

1. *Get your uniform on.* Soldiers are identified by their uniforms. Spies and undercover agents disguise themselves, hoping to slip in without being noticed. The Lord doesn't need undercover Christians, but those who wear his uniform and proudly identify themselves with him.

Do you act as a "secret believer"—one who unveils your Christianity only when it is non-threatening, then in more hostile situations, covers up your true identity? This kind of clandestine discipleship makes it easy to deny the Lord in difficult times. When the apostle Peter tried to secretly follow the Lord at a distance, on three occasions he denied that he knew Jesus.

To come out of your foxhole, you must first decide to be identified with Jesus Christ as your Lord and Savior. No more secrecy, no more undercover discipleship. Straightforwardly proclaiming your allegiance to the Lord is practical evidence of saving faith. Christ identified with your sins, taking them upon himself. By faith, you identify with his righteousness. After you accept Christ as your Savior and Lord, then publicly profess your faith.

Christians are clothed with garments of righteousness and wear helmets of salvation. Put on the uniform, then. Identify yourself publicly as a disciple of Jesus Christ.

2. *Rally to the cause.* Moses stood in the gate of the camp and said to the children of Israel,

"Whoever is for the Lord, come to me!" (Exod. 32:26). It is not enough to be identified with the Lord; you must be identified with his people. That means be involved—not only with a church, but with a Bible club, prayer group or wherever God's people gather. It doesn't mean you have to reject all your old friends, but you need to join those who are raising the standard of Christianity in your school, your neighborhood or your workplace.

3. *Give yourself to God for service.* Perhaps you want to take a stand for Christ, but find yourself held back by things in your life that need to change. If the Holy Spirit convicts you of compromise and hypocrisy, ask the Lord to forgive you and cleanse you with his blood.

Dedicate yourself wholly to him, and give him every aspect of your life, to be used in his service.

Who is going to raise the standard of Christ? I am. And so are you!

A whole army of committed Christians is on

the rise, and in the pages that follow you can learn how they are arising over the darkness that threatens to swallow our land. With the power of the risen Christ and the encouragement of others, you *can* become one of God's standard-bearers, and retake your world for him.

2

WHY IS EVERYONE SO UPSET?
(They're Plotting Together Against the Lord)

A Stage of Rage

Who can forget seeing the videotape of Reginald Denny as he was dragged out of his truck and almost killed during the Los Angeles riots in 1992? I wince every time I remember seeing that young man throw a brick and hit Denny in the head, just to release his own frustration and rage.

The same thing happened to a young Christian named Stephen. Hearing him preach the gospel so enraged the Jews that they stoned him to death. The book of Acts describes their terrifying frame of mind:

> **. . . they were furious and gnashed their teeth at [Stephen] . . . At this they covered their ears and, yelling at the top of their voices, they all rushed at him. (Acts 7:54, 57)**

Take it back a little farther. Three Jewish slaves serving in King Nebuchadnezzar's court were promoted to be administrators. Shadrach, Meshach and Abednego were their names. They refused to bow and worship the king's image even when threatened with being burned in the fiery furnace. Instead, they followed their convictions and let the chips fall where they might. As I said in the last chapter, this kind of commitment is what sets us apart—and these guys were unbelievable heroes of the faith.

All of us have known people who thought the world revolved around them. Nebuchadnezzar was one of those people. He had a real attitude, especially when someone didn't bow down and worship his false god. Here's how he responded to people who lived by their convictions:

Furious with rage, Nebuchadnezzar summoned Shadrach, Meshach and Abednego . . . (Dan. 3:13)

He threatened them some more, but they would not be intimidated. They continued to take a stand for the Lord, which only made him madder.

Then Nebuchadnezzar was furious with Shadrach, Meshach and Abednego, and his attitude toward them changed. He ordered the furnace heated seven times hotter than usual. (Dan. 3:19)

You may be thinking like I am—making the furnace seven times hotter would only hasten their deaths. If Nebuchadnezzar wanted to cause them pain, that doesn't make sense. But when people get *that* mad, sometimes the things they do don't make a lot of sense.

Take a look around us, and you'll see what I mean.

The Influence of Antichrist

As director of High School Ministries Network in Wichita, Kansas, Cheryl Hurley developed a good working relationship with the public school system in Wichita. In the Fall of 1993, High School Ministries Network planned to bring in speakers to give motivational talks at the local schools. The talks they would give at these school assemblies were not religious, but simply a dynamic motivational message that inspired students to work hard, stay off drugs and set their expectations high. Afterwards, students would be invited to Christian meetings that would take place in the evenings. All the planning and promotion was going well until one individual decided that no Christian speaker should have the right to say anything in the public schools.

This individual tried protesting. When that didn't work, he tried to get the local ACLU involved. Even the ACLU saw no grounds for action. The national ACLU finally was contacted, and, consequently, the speakers were threatened. If they mentioned God in the assemblies, they would face a lawsuit from the ACLU.

What is the big deal anyway? A lot of things happening today just don't make sense. Why? Because there is a spirit in the world that causes people to lose touch with reason and logic as they passionately oppose Christ. Satanism, witchcraft and other occultic groups have, of course, always been decidedly anti-Christ—that is, *against Christ*. But now that same hatred of Christ is infecting areas of our society that directly affect all of us.

In America, for instance, our leading educational institutions were established to glorify God. Harvard, Yale, Princeton and all but a handful of the first hundred colleges were founded as specifically Christian institutions. One of their main purposes for being was to train ministers of the gospel.

In 1892, the U.S. Supreme Court made an exhaustive study of the supposed connection between Christianity and the government of the United States. After reviewing hundreds of volumes of historical documents, the Court asserted, "These references . . . add a volume of unofficial declarations to the mass of organic utterances that this is a religious people . . . a Christian nation." Likewise, in 1931, Supreme Court Justice George Sutherland reviewed the 1892 decision in reference to another case, and openly declared that Americans are a "Christian people." And in 1952, Justice William O. Douglas affirmed that "we are a religious people and our institutions presuppose a Supreme Being."[1]

Nevertheless, in America today, as in other Western nations, both government and education now have taken up that same anti-Christian banner.

A school near Orlando, Florida, set out with a vengeance to ban the Christian celebration of Christmas. When middle-school student Jill Reichert, as part of a school Christmas art contest, drew a nativity scene to adorn the door of her classroom, her teacher made her tear it down, citing the "separation of church and state."[2]

A public high school senior in Atlanta recently was suspended for passing a handwritten note to a fellow student in the hallway. Containing—what? Information about a drug deal? A gang war? No. The note merely gave the time and place of the next Fellowship of Christian Athletes meeting. The student who received the note was given a written reprimand from authorities, stating that any further possession of "Christian material" could lead to suspension.

Another school principal told a parent that students could not bring Bibles to school or wear religious T-shirts, buttons or other Christian symbols.[3]

In May 1990, when students in another school handed out about 1,000 copies of a Christian newspaper, *Issues and Answers,* school officials responded angrily. They confiscated the paper and detained the students. One of those students subsequently had his school meritorious service award taken away by school authorities.[4]

Jack Gaddis, a U.S. serviceman, faced court martial charges for going door-to-door in officers' housing on his base, inviting people to come to his church and witnessing to interested persons.[5]

The manager of a Chevrolet dealership on the West Coast was fired for refusing to attend a management seminar that clearly was an indoctrination into New Age religious philosophies.[6]

If these were isolated incidents, perhaps we could shrug them off. But thousands of such cases occur every day, as Christians are confronted by business people, educators or government officials who unwittingly are motivated by the spirit of antichrist. And in many of these cases, believers are refusing to be intimidated. They are taking a stand and prevailing. Laws and regulations are being challenged and changed, and Christians are winning back the rights that were ours to begin with.

The point is this: *Someone has to take a stand.*

Why for centuries have people tried to discredit the Bible? Why have Christians been persecuted throughout history? Why is it politically correct to believe anything you want about God and to live any way you choose—as long as you don't believe in Jesus Christ or the Bible, or traditional Christian values? Why is everyone so upset about Christians?

They're Not Really Mad at You

Here's the answer: At the root of our sinful nature, we are at war with God and with anything that reminds us of God.

My early experiences helped me understand this. The youngest of three children, I grew up in a lower-middle-class neighborhood in Trenton, New Jersey. Across the street from my house was a wooded area with a creek running through it. Gang kids hung out over there, smoking dope and sniffing glue. I always had to be careful—it was dangerous to go through the woods to another neighborhood. To get through safely, you had to know somebody, or be with somebody. For me, it was *really* dangerous, because of my brother Mario.

Mario, my big brother, got married when he was nineteen. I was eleven, and that left me to spend my teenage years alone around people that my brother had previously beaten up. Mario was a cool dresser and the toughest guy in the neighborhood. His knuckles always were bruised from fights he'd been in. Now there were guys who wanted to kill *me*—not because I had done anything to them, but because I looked like Mario, acted like him, had the same mannerisms and the same last name and I lived in the same house. I reminded them of someone who beat them up years before.

"Don't be surprised if the world hates you," Jesus said. "They hated me first." We Christians are made in the likeness and image of God. So we remind the devil of someone who, two thousand years ago, beat him up and tossed him out of heaven, and then crushed his head. We haven't done anything to him, but we identify and associate with someone who opposes their sinful, rebellious lifestyles.

Left to ourselves, we want to be our own God, to free ourselves from moral restraints, and to rid the world of a God who pronounces judgment upon our sin. Listen to how one of America's greatest early preachers, Jonathan Edwards, put it:

> *Natural men are greater enemies to God than any other being whatsoever. There is no other being that so stands in a sinner's way as God. Men hate their enemies in proportion to two things: 1) the degree of opposition to what they look on as their own interests, 2) and their power and ability to oppose them. A great and powerful opponent is more hated than a weak, impotent one, and there is none more powerful than God.*[7]

Unless you've been hiding from the world on a desert island for the last twenty years, you probably can imagine the modern-day response to those quotes from Edwards:

"Why, that's old-fashioned thinking! We reject this pessimistic view of humans."

"We hold a modern and progressive view of people."

"We affirm and celebrate the beauty of the enlightened human spirit."

So-called "enlightened" people like to claim how tolerant they are. But if you don't think humans have a sinful nature at war with God, try this: Sit down with leaders of Planned Parenthood, ACLU, the Coalition of Gays and Lesbians, a liberal church denomination or many educators and make the following statements:

I believe the Bible is the Word of God.

I believe in absolute standards of morality.

I believe Jesus Christ is the one way to salvation.

I believe the unborn fetus is a human being with rights.

I believe sex outside of marriage is wrong and constitutes fornication and adultery.

I believe homosexuality is one of the final stages of moral perversion.

I believe America was established as a Christian nation, founded by Christians on the principles of the Bible.

I believe God will judge America, not in heaven but in this life, for its sin.

I believe in a real heaven and a real hell.

Watch the response. I think you'll see that Edwards was right. (If you're going to try this, I suggest you stand close to the door and have someone outside waiting with the motor running!)

Plotting Together Against the Lord

There is a reason Christianity is violently opposed in our world while other religions and philosophies are tolerated. It has to do with a political agenda that goes all the way back to our beginnings.

Why do the heathen rage, and the people imagine a vain thing? The kings of the earth set themselves, and the rulers take counsel together, against the Lord, and against his anointed, saying "Let us break their bands asunder, and cast away their cords from us." (Ps. 2:1-3, KJV)

Biblical Christianity evokes violent responses from some people, because only in Christianity is there an absolute right and wrong. People hate the Bible and Christianity because of the law of God. Again, listen to Jonathan Edwards:

Natural men are enemies to God's dominion, and their nature shows their good will to dethrone Him if they could. They would be glad if there were no God and would cause it to be so if they could. Their heart says, "Let the world be empty of a God, for He stands in my way."[8]

33

God's righteousness and his unchangeable law make Christianity a stumbling block for many. Organizations and individuals carry a political and moral agenda that aims to remove all obstacles to their sin. Their goal is to "break [God's] bands asunder and cast away his cords." They counsel together to rid themselves of the law of God; anyone who preaches the gospel or stands for righteousness stands in the way of their agenda.

For example, take a look at the agenda and policies of the National Education Association (NEA) to see if they are compatible with biblical Christianity:

The NEA strongly supports the hiring of homosexual teachers.

The NEA is opposed to voluntary prayer in schools.

The NEA advocates putting school-based clinics, with contraceptive services and abortion referrals, in public schools.

The NEA opposes home schooling, merit pay for teachers and parental choice of schools. (The NEA spent $1 million to oppose school choice when it was put on the California ballot as Proposition 174.)

In short, the NEA can be characterized as a liberal political action organization that has gained control of the public schools in America.

To get an idea of the extent to which they want to wrestle away from parents the rights to shape the values and philosophy of the next generation, listen to what *Forbes* magazine said about the "power goals" of the NEA. The NEA is pushing an agenda that includes:

•early childhood education programs in the public schools for children from birth through age eight.

•guidance and counseling programs integrated into the entire education system, beginning at the pre-kindergarten level.

•"the right of every individual to live in an environment of freely available information, knowledge, and wisdom about sexuality."

•"immediate, direct, and confidential access to health, social, and psychological services."

The NEA aims to take away parents' ability to teach their values to their children, so that children can be indoctrinated from the earliest ages with anti-Christian, secular humanist propaganda.[9]

In 1981, Suzanne Clark, a Bristol, Tennessee, mom, wrote a letter to the editor of her local newspaper charging that the NEA promoted secular humanism in the public school. The NEA sued Suzanne Clark. Her defense was that her letter was true.

Her lawyer, Michael Farris, took depositions from the highest officials at the NEA. He also had access to a number of their files and documents. As he researched the case, he began to uncover evidence that Suzanne Clark's letter was accurate, and that the heart of the NEA's agenda is indeed to promote in public schools a secular humanist philosophy contrary to and intolerant of Christianity. Faced with overwhelming evidence, the NEA dropped the suit, it appears, lest their agenda be revealed.[10]

Whether leaders of these organizations know it or not, they are plotting together against the Lord. Why? Because when you place yourself outside God's law you set yourself up to speak and act according to the spirit that opposes God. This can be true of anyone. When James and John wanted to call down fire and destroy people, for instance, Jesus said to them, **"Ye know not what manner of spirit ye are of"** **(Luke 9:55, KJV)**. You see, our true enemies are not people, but spiritual principalities and powers that motivate them and shape their perspectives.

Nobody Likes Being Hated

The spirit of this world has always been the enemy of righteousness and the violent persecutor of the Lord's Anointed. So you shouldn't be surprised when you run into opposition. Jesus warned his disciples that it would be like this.

> **If the world hates you, keep in mind that it hated me first. If you belonged to the world, it would love you as its own. As it is, you do not belong to the world, but I have chosen you out of the world. That is why the world hates you. Remember the words I spoke to you: "No servant is greater than his master." If they persecuted me, they will persecute you also. If they obeyed my teaching, they will obey yours also. (John 15:18-20)**

Terry Law and the music group, Living Sound, traveled and ministered in the Soviet bloc countries for many years before the Iron Curtain came down. One young Estonian Christian, Viktor, risked his life many times on their behalf. In 1979, Viktor was assisting the team on a tour. As always, they were followed by the KGB. They did not technically break any rules, but they were unwelcome visitors and the KGB agents were waiting for them to make a mistake.

At one point during the trip, Viktor stepped onto the Living Sound bus. At that time it was against the law for nationals to be on foreign tour buses. Immediately the KGB came after Viktor. Members of the Living Sound team stepped in front of the agents, asked them the time and tried to occupy them while Viktor fled.

Later, when they met up again in secret, Terry Law said to Viktor, "If you keep on like this you'll wind up in prison or dead."

Viktor looked at him for a moment, then replied with a smile, "When I gave my life to Jesus Christ, I died. That is what scripture teaches. So I am not afraid. You cannot kill a person twice."

Viktor eventually was arrested and spent several years in a Soviet prison for his faith.

There will always be some who are influenced and dominated by the spirit of this world. You and I will face opposition from them. Some of these people may not even be part of the twenty percent group of the committed opponents of Christianity. Rather, they are everyday people who do their own thing—until the subject of Jesus Christ or Christianity comes up. Then you see them go into a rage.

Facing angry opposition is simply part of being a disciple of Jesus Christ. Realize that from the beginning, and don't be surprised when it happens. Jesus said that we are blessed if we are persecuted for the sake of righteousness, not self-righteousness (Matt. 5:10). We don't wave our "righteousness" in other people's faces, though. Apart from the blood of Jesus Christ, we all stand guilty, without hope. Jesus also said that we would be blessed if they accuse us falsely (Matt. 5:11). That's why we need to make sure we're living what we preach and give no one cause to accuse us.

Don't draw fire as a result of your overbearing attitude. If you are persecuted, be sure it is for your love of Christ.

The real test of discipleship, however, is not whether we are persecuted. When people hate us and falsely accuse us, our natural tendency is to return their fire. But it doesn't matter if they shoot first—true righteousness is revealed in how we respond.

> **You have heard that it was said, "Love your neighbor and hate your enemy." But I tell you: Love your enemies and pray for those who persecute you, that you may be sons of your Father in heaven. (Matt. 5:43-45)**

Jesus was patient under fire, and he did not hold the sins of his persecutors against them. **"Forgive them, for they do not know what they are doing,"** he said **(Luke 23:34)**. Stephen proved himself a disciple of Christ when he cried with a loud voice as they stoned him, **"Lord, do not hold this sin against them" (Acts 7:60)**.

It's easy to love those who love you back. Pagans do that. But the supernatural love of Christ is evident when you love those who hate you, persecute you and despitefully use you. It's not enough to be right—the love of Christ also must shine through you.

The Unstoppable Gospel

There have always been those who oppose God's plan and

purpose, those who plot against the Lord and against his Anointed. But history and the Word of God tell us that the gospel is unstoppable! In fact, in times of persecution, it flourishes.

The psalmist tells us the Lord's response to those in authority who counsel together to cast off all restraints:

> **The One enthroned in heaven laughs; the Lord scoffs at them. Then he rebukes them in his anger . . . I will proclaim the decree of the Lord: He said to me, "You are my Son; today I have become your Father. Ask of me, and I will make the nations your inheritance, the ends of the earth your possession." (Ps. 2:4-8)**

God laughs at the efforts of those who work feverishly to keep Christians quiet, to keep prayer and Bible studies out of schools and to tear down the restraints of moral law. He's laughing— because the spread of the gospel cannot be stopped. It will reach to every nation, even to the ends of the earth.

Former director of High School Ministries Network in Wichita Cheryl Hurley didn't let the passionate opposition of a few individuals stop her. She contacted the American Center for Law and Justice (ACLJ). Attorney Joel Thornton counseled her to take advantage of what opportunities she had and trust God to do the rest. So she continued with her plan. In the assembly programs, speakers kept within the guidelines of the ACLU, never mentioning God or the evening Christian meetings. The students themselves invited friends, and passed out handbills and buttons with the program's slogan, *Locker to Locker.* Over 15,000 showed for the evening programs to listen to Christian musicians and to hear the gospel preached without compromise. Many students gave their lives to Jesus Christ in those meetings.

The Pharisees and Sadducees also conspired together to stop the spread of the gospel. They crucified Jesus, arrested and flogged Peter and John, threatened them, ordered them to stop talking about Jesus and finally had James beheaded. They sent Saul to Damascus to track down, arrest and imprison Christians who had fled from Jerusalem. They dispatched men throughout Asia Minor to dispute the preaching of Paul.

But it didn't work. They couldn't stop the gospel from spreading. Nothing could.

Despite problems and divisions in the Jerusalem church, the death of Ananias and Sapphira, the stoning of Stephen, imprisonments, shipwrecks, confrontation with the occult, riots, mobs and every kind of opposition—nothing could stop the spread of the gospel.

Not much has changed since that time. For over fifty years, the church in China has endured terrific persecution. But the provinces where Christians suffered the most during the Cultural Revolution are those that now report the most consistent harvest of souls for God.

In the last few years the Chinese government has intensified its persecutions and declared war on Jesus Christ. In the Henan Province, officials made this decree: "It was you Christians who brought down the regimes in Eastern Europe and the Soviet Union, but here in China we will stop you now!" In this same province, church growth has been so remarkable that Communist Party bosses refer to the area as the "Jesus Nest." In one region, a contingent of 260,000 believers has grown to about 600,000 during the last ten years.

In the Szechwan Province, where one out of forty people on earth live, nearly two thousand new churches have been started over the last three years, despite fierce government resistance.

In the aftermath of the 1989 Tiananmen Square massacre, the churches face persecution not seen since the Cultural Revolution. In China, believers regularly are arrested, fined, beaten and imprisoned—all part of the price of following Jesus Christ.

Yet, the gospel is unstoppable.

A September 1992 bulletin released by the Beijing Statistical Bureau acknowledged that there were seventy-five million Chinese Christians residing in the country. That is triple the membership of the Communist Party![11]

Nations, organizations and individuals continue to plot together against the Lord—maybe against you, too. Some individuals hiss like a viper whenever Jesus Christ is mentioned. What should be our response to all that? *Rejoice and be glad!* Remember, if Christ is lifted up—regardless of the opposition—he will draw all people to himself.

With the rise of people and groups committed to putting Christ down, the question for us is, *Who is going to lift him up?*

I've heard people say that the last page of the Book says we win. That's great, but our victory does not have to wait until the last page of the Bible is fulfilled. The spread of the gospel is unstoppable now. . . if Christ is lifted up.

Time 2
Toughen Up

No one likes being hated, criticized or ridiculed. We try to avoid pain as much as possible. But you can't control what other people do. What you can do, what you must do, is make some decisions and set some priorities for yourself. By doing so, you set your own course rather than being manipulated by the opinions and intimidation of other people.

1. Don't let other people determine who you are. Be your own person. Do what's right. Believe what's true.

2. Here's the priority I've set in my life: *I'm more concerned about what God thinks of me than what others think of me. It matters more to me that I do what is right than what is popular.* I challenge you to take that same stand.

3. Look at what you do and say from God's perspective. Ask yourself, "How is this going to look to God?" Not only will this priority cause you to live a life more pleasing to God, but it also will enhance your self-respect. Those who waiver and

waffle under the opinions and pressures of other people usually wind up hating themselves. Your own integrity is your greatest possession. Don't let anyone steal it from you.

4. Don't be pushed around. Stand your ground. Some people are intent on denying Christians their religious freedoms and their freedom of speech. American citizens need to know their rights. I highly recommend that every believer get a copy of *Knowing Your Rights* by Jay Sekulow. This booklet outlines what you need to know about the law and your rights. To obtain a copy, write to:

Liberty, Life and Family
P.O. Box 65248
Virginia Beach, VA 23467-5248

If you experience conflict with school or public officials over a matter of religious expression, contact:

American Center for Law and Justice
P.O. Box 64429
Virginia Beach, VA 23467
(phone) 804/523-7570

Others you can contact include:

Christian Solidarity International
Secretariat
P.O. Box 881
CH- 8029
Zurich, SWITZERLAND

Rutherford Institute
P.O. Box 7482
Charlottesville, VA 22906-7482

3

DARKNESS IS SPREADING EVERYWHERE
(But the Devil Always Goes Too Far)

Try standing on any street corner in Russia with a sign that reads, "I know something about God. Stop here." Traffic will back up for blocks and a large crowd will gather. You don't have to be a gifted preacher or have a music group to attract attention. Simply explain the gospel and hundreds of people will receive Christ as their Savior, because throughout the former Soviet Union people are starving for God.

Compare that with the spiritual apathy, unbelief and hardheartedness of the American public. You begin to wonder, *Is there hope for America?*

The answer is yes, and it's not wishful thinking that tells us so. There are good reasons for believing that the standard of Christianity will again be raised in America.

It's difficult to march into battle if we think we have no chance of winning. When God tells you to take a stand, your first thought may be: "Is this going to do any good?" No one wants to give their all to a losing cause. That's why it's important to know that our prayers and hopes for revival are valid.

Things around us seem out of control. It appears the forces of darkness are winning. Revival *is* going to come, but things will probably get worse before they get better.

In order to fight off discouragement and keep standing strong in the face of opposition, we need to understand two things: 1) the judgment of God and 2) the weakness of Satan.

The "Judgment Thing"

Few things infuriate modern pseudo-intellectuals and secular humanists like talk of God's judgment on individuals and nations.

"How could you believe in such a cruel God?" they ask.

Opponents of righteousness often believe in a form of religion and even talk about their faith in God—but it's a "politically correct" religion. Praying and having faith are okay, they say, as long as God does not hold us accountable to a moral standard.

All religious beliefs or gods are acceptable—except the God of the Bible. Richard Geer, along with California Senator Diane Feinstein, recently co-hosted a dinner in Los Angeles honoring the Dalai Lama. Meg Ryan and Geer's wife, Cindy Crawford, as well as other actors attended the gala, which raised $250,000 for the American Himalayan Foundation. Hinduism, Buddhism, any kind of 'ism is cool in Hollywood—just don't mention Jesus Christ.[1]

The greatest sin of the '90s, according to the philosophy of this age, is not murder, rape or robbery. People who commit such crimes are now considered victims of society. The greatest sin of our age is intolerance or putting someone else down. You can believe in Jesus—just don't say he is the only way. You can believe in a god—but not our holy and righteous God.

It's that "judgment thing" that upsets folks. People hate the standard of God's righteousness so they attempt to pull it down and make God like themselves.

"We believe in the fatherhood of God and the brotherhood of man," say liberal church leaders. These are code words for a warm fuzzy god who would never challenge how we live or what we believe.

God *is* a God of love, mercy and patience—but never lose sight of the fact that he also is a holy and righteous God who will sooner or later judge us all.

> *America's dead and dying hand is on the threshold*
> *   of the Church*
> *While the spirit of Sodom and Gomorrah vex us all.*
> *When it gets to the point where people would rather*
> *Come out of the closet than clean it,*
> *It's the sign that the judgment of God is gonna fall.*
>
> ("American Again," by Carman and
> Michael Omartian)

Sins of the Mind

The wrath of God is being revealed from heaven against all the godlessness and wickedness of men

who suppress the truth by their wickedness, since what may be known about God is plain to them, because God has made it plain to them. For since the creation of the world God's invisible qualities—his eternal power and divine nature—have been clearly seen, being understood from what has been made, so that men are without excuse. (Rom. 1:18-20)

All of us, Christians and non-Christians alike, feel the conviction of the Holy Spirit when we sin. We are made in the image of God, and our consciences warn us when we violate the moral law of God.

But we tend to play mental games with the Holy Spirit to try to get around the conviction of sin. Some Christians take drugs, or sleep around, and try to justify it. "Well, I've made a rule," they say. "I don't *deal* drugs, and I don't take anything that will really mess up my mind." Or, "I only sleep with someone I really, really love." These are weak attempts to replace God's laws with their own. It will never work.

What should we do when the Holy Spirit convicts us? Simply, we repent. But sin is addicting, and some are so attached to their sins they would rather run the risk of going to hell than to part with them.

Those who are not Christians deal with conviction and guilt by saying to themselves: "There is no God—and if there is no God, then there is no guilt or judgment. These guilty feelings are only that—feelings imposed upon me by an old-fashioned society."

Good try, but that won't work with God! The Word of God says this about those who suppress the truth in unrighteousness: "They are without excuse."

Jesus said:

This is the verdict: Light has come into the world, but men loved darkness instead of light because their deeds were evil. Everyone who does evil hates the light, and will not come into the light for fear that his deeds will be exposed. (John 3:19-20)

Have It Your Way

You've heard it said, "Be careful what you ask for—you might get it." That may be truer than we realize. God is patient and long-suffering, giving people time to turn from their evil ways. Though judgment is slow in coming, it will certainly arrive if they continue in their sin.

Romans 1 says that God gave evil men over to the lust of their hearts and to degrading passions. He gave them over to fulfill in their bodies the lust that was in their hearts. Consequently, they degenerated into deeper levels of sexual perversion. God's judgment on them was removing his grace that prevented them from going further into sin. In other words, God "gave them over" by removing his restraining hand.

Not only were they given over to their own lusts, they were given over to depraved minds. In a depraved mind, right and wrong have been reversed. That's why the standards of right and wrong morality in our society are so bizarre. When you reject God and his law, you are on the way to ethical and moral insanity.

Here are a few examples of depraved thinking:

A private Catholic hospital in Oak Park, Illinois, was blocked from erecting a cross on its own smokestack, because of potential offense to local residents.[2] Yet homosexuals are granted the right to march in New York's St. Patrick's Day Parade.

A Decatur, Illinois, primary-school teacher discovered the word *God* in a phonics textbook. She ordered the seven-year-olds to strike it out, saying that it is against the law to mention God in a public school.[3] Has it become unconstitutional to teach students to spell the word *God*?

In 1988, the California legislature considered a bill on sex education for public schools that required that

> *course material and instructions shall stress that monogamous heterosexual intercourse [one man and one woman] within marriage is a traditional American value.*

The senator promoting the bill received a letter of protest from the ACLU that included this passage:

> *It is our position that monogamous, heterosexual intercourse within marriage as a traditional American value is an unconstitutional establishment of a religious doctrine in public schools. There are various religions which hold contrary beliefs with respect to marriage*

and monogamy. We believe [this bill] violates the First Amendment.[4]

People today seem to think it is unconstitutional to teach anything that even *agrees with* the beliefs of Christianity. Their alternative is to make the entire curriculum anti-moral and anti-Christian.

George Washington, in his farewell address, warned about this kind of depraved and perverted thinking:

> *And let us with caution indulge the supposition that morality may be maintained without religion. Whatever may be conceded to the influence of refined education on minds . . . reason and experience both forbid us to expect that national morality can prevail in exclusion of religious principle.*[5]

When the Supreme Court decided not long ago that it was unconstitutional to hang a copy of the Ten Commandments in a Kentucky classroom, it reflected what many had already decided. Now we are seeing the firstfruits of a generation that does not even know the difference between right and wrong.

"We'll decide for ourselves what's right and wrong," people declare. "We will not be restrained by God's law." As the haters of the Lord said, in Psalms 2, **"Let us tear their fetters apart, and cast away their cords from us" (Ps. 2:3, KJV).**

At some point God will say, "All right, have it your way." He will remove the restraining grace, and give them over to perversion and depraved minds.

Paul wrote to the Corinthian church:

> **Hand this man over to Satan, so that the sinful nature may be destroyed and his spirit saved on the day of the Lord. (1 Cor. 5:5)**

God removes his restraining grace in order to bring an individual to repentance. He also removes the restraints from a society that has rejected him so that the resulting chaos and barbarism will cause them to turn back.

In Jesus' parable of the Prodigal, the son got what he demanded, but it destroyed him, leaving him to eat what the pigs did not want. Only when he got desperate did he repent and go back to his father. The nature of God's judgment upon a rebellious people gives them over to their own desires. The purpose of God's judgment in this life is always that it will, in the end, bring us to our senses. So, in fact, much of the moral perversion and depraved thinking that we see today is the result of God giving our society over to its own desires.

That doesn't mean he's given up on the world. He's just giving the devil enough rope to hang himself. Dawn always follows darkness.

The Devil Can't Help Himself

Lucifer wanted to ascend to the throne and reign in heaven. God rejected Lucifer and cast him out of heaven, but he fixed his love upon humanity and gave us the promise of reigning forever with him. Perhaps then it is jealousy that fuels Satan's persistent, passionate and uncontrollable hatred for humanity through the ages.

Pastor and author Mark Rutland provides an interesting insight into one of Satan's major downfalls:

> *Satan has never had any self-control and no ability to know when to stop. His tactics will always become more and more brutal, more lethal, more horrible and more up-front. He always goes too far, the result being whole nations desperately seeking to get back to God.*[6]

That's what happened with Israel's most wicked king, Ahaz. He spent his sixteen-year reign leading the nation into the depths of depravity. Ahaz was the latest in a long line of kings, each of whom had done more wickedness than his father before him. The moral and spiritual life of Israel was about as low as it could get. Idol worship, pagan religions, human sacrifices and every kind of immorality and perversion permeated the society. They had cast off all restraints (2 Chron. 28).

When Ahaz died, surely the people said to themselves, "If the father was this perverted, how much worse will the son be? If the nation has declined this much in one generation, how bad will it be in the next?" Using his servant, Ahaz, Satan pushed the nation to the edge of total depravity. The national and spiritual climate were so polluted that there seemed to be no hope.

Then, this new kid ascended to the throne.

A Holy Rebellion

Young Hezekiah's moral ladder by all rights should have had the rungs knocked out of it. But in his first act as king, he stepped up to the throne and said, "We're going to have a revival in this country. The Lord has put it in my heart to return to God."

How did this happen? Based on his father's influence, he should have been completely depraved. Hezekiah was not a likely candidate to turn a nation to God— but, you see, the devil had pushed too hard.

There is no person on earth who cannot be touched by the Holy Spirit. Again, Mark Rutland says,

> *As Hezekiah walked the hallways of his father's palace, which was filled with harlotry, perversion, sodomy, brutality and even human sacrifice, something happened. Hezekiah's soul hung over the abyss, and he could have gone one of two ways. He could have followed in his father's footsteps deeper and deeper into the pit of depravity. Instead it went the other way, and something inside said, "I wasn't born for this."*

Listen, parents, you may have a kid at home who's driving you nuts. He may look you right in the face and with rebellion in his voice, tell you where to get off and that you can take your God with you. This same kid could one day stand up to a society that is drenched in evil, pornography and wretched rebellion and say, "You don't tell me how to live. I'm going to live for God."

We are way too timid toward our society. We must integrate into our lives a *holy rebellion*.

To the ungodly influences of the world that try to shape us in their image, we need to say, "You don't tell me what to think. You don't tell me what my values are. You don't tell me how to dress. You don't tell me how to worship. I *will* serve the Lord."

That's what Hezekiah said to his generation. "We're going to seek God," he said. "You priests are dirty. The temple is dirty. The city, the nation and our lives are dirty, too."

They could have killed him. But the people were thrilled to see someone with guts enough to raise the standard.

It may look to you like Satan is driving our land straight to hell. We see immoral leaders who pass evil laws. All of it will play right into the hands of God. It may come to a point that our heads-down, cowardly submission to evil will bring us to where someone jumps out of a foxhole, raises the standard and says, "This is not what we were born for."

Down and Out, Broken and Busted

When Satan goes too far in his efforts to corrupt and destroy the human race, the results are similar to what we see now in the former Soviet Union.

The former Soviet Union is busted. They should put a sign on the border that says, "Country Out of Order." The infrastructures and the buildings are falling down, the government is in chaos and the economy is dead. Nothing works. Everything in the country is broken.

Satan attempts to destroy believers' faith and steal their hope. But in doing so he creates in them a need for hope and faith in eternal things. He succeeds in creating an insatiable hunger for God!

But how far is too far? When Stalin was murdering millions, was that going too far? No, it wasn't. Were the oppressions of the Soviet KGB under Khrushchev and Brezhnev going too far? No, but their days were numbered.

An Unlikely Reformer

Mikhail Gorbachev spent his life climbing up the complex system of Soviet bureaucracy. His mentor for many years was Mikhail Suslov, the ideological minister for Leonid Brezhnev. A less-likely candidate than Gorbachev to lead a revival in the USSR could not be imagined.

But shortly after Gorbachev ascended to the seat of power, he stood in front of a microphone and said, in effect, we've been wrong about Communism and world domination—what do you say we tear down the Berlin wall? I never thought I'd see such a thing in my lifetime! And it didn't take a period of years or even months to accomplish. They were talking about it on CNN one night, and the bulldozers were tearing down the wall practically the next day.

As Satan pushes America and other western nations deeper into legislative and cultural depravity, I believe that he will push us so far that our society will eventually have to say our only hope is in God.

When it seems we are rapidly skidding off the moral road and into the ditch, don't be discouraged and don't panic. It may be that more people will finally discover their need to serve God.

Bright Lights, Deep Darkness

When Jesus heard that John the Baptist had been thrown into prison, he left home and went to the region of Zebulun and Naphtali. Matthew tells us the reason:

> **To fulfill what was said through the prophet Isaiah: "Land of Zebulun and land of Naphtali, the way to the sea, along the Jordan, Galilee of the Gentiles— the people living in darkness have seen a great light; on those living in the land of the shadow of death a light has dawned." (Matt. 4:14-16)**

Jesus went to the people who sat in darkness. The great news is that he's continued to do that to this day. We're not the first civilization to descend into godless darkness. Even in America, young as we are, we can already see God's faithfulness to us as a nation. Listen to this story of a near disaster early in our history.

The spiritual battles being fought in the early 1800s in America were, in many ways, similar to those we face today. Sidney Alhstrom, one of the most respected historians of American Christianity wrote concerning the darkness of that period: "God seemed almost to have withdrawn his blessing from New England, and above all from those who most cherished 'true' doctrine."[7]

In place of this *true doctrine* came the discouraging rise of anti-Christian organizations—the Universalists, the Unitarians and the

Deists. All of them denied the fundamental teachings of Christianity (such as the deity of Christ, his atoning blood, his resurrection and the Bible as God's Word). During this time, an edition of Thomas Paine's heretical book, *Age of Reason,* was published in France and sold in America for a few cents, and where it could not be sold, it was given away.[8]

Paine declared that the Old and New Testaments were unworthy of a good God. "It would be more consistent that we call it the word of a demon than the word of God," Paine blasted.[9]

This one book had disastrous effects on American colleges. Students looking for an excuse to rebel against the society of their day embraced the new "religion" of rationalism. They held mock communion services and called themselves by the names of famous skeptics and outspoken unbelievers. Christian students became such a minority that on some campuses they felt compelled to meet secretly.[10]

On the frontier there also was great concern. The church was not keeping up with the vast movement westward. An Episcopal preacher described the Carolinas: "How many thousands . . . never saw, much less read, or even heard a chapter of the Bible! . . . [How many] have never heard the name of Christ, save in curses!"[11]

Peter Cartwright, a Methodist preacher, described the situation in Logan County, Kentucky: "Here, many refugees from almost all parts of the Union fled to escape justice of punishment . . . It was a desperate state of society. Murderers, horse-thieves, highway robbers, and counterfeiters fled there, until they combined and actually formed a majority."[12]

As new states sprang up to join the Union, church leaders faced the frightening prospect that the raw wilderness was an ungodly force, threatening to bring a moral breakdown to the entire nation.[13]

Historian Timothy Dwight wrote that the two decades following the Revolutionary War were "the period of the lowest ebb-tide of vitality in the history of American Christianity"[14] For true believers, it was a sad, dark day. The spirit of infidelity seemed to be rising. Was judgment about to come to a young and backslidden nation?

Just when it looked like the days were numbered for Christianity in America, a new light burst forth in the midst of darkness. And the effects on the nation—and around the world—were titanic.

In the West one of history's great awakenings began with James McGready, an eighteenth-century preacher, and spread throughout North Carolina. Other faithful preachers such as Barton Stone and Peter Cartwright were used by God as the awakening spread like wildfire. McGready and his colleagues planned a camp-meeting revival to be held in late July 1800 at Gasper River in Logan County, Kentucky—in the heart of spiritual darkness. Over 8,000 people arrived, coming from distances as great as one hundred miles, to pray and seek God again!

That was just the beginning. In 1801, the largest city in Kentucky, Lexington, had a population of 1,800. Yet that year, the Cane Ridge camp-meeting revivals held near Lexington drew between 10,000 and 20,000 people!

This spiritual awakening eventually spread to New England.

When Charles Finney opened evangelistic meetings in the town of Western, New York, in October of 1825, it touched off seven years of the most intense evangelistic activity America has ever seen. From this tiny town, the awakening spread throughout the nation. Light shined again, and the darkness could not withstand it.

Similar accounts can be told concerning spiritual darkness that preceded other great revivals. It happened in England before Wesley, and in Germany before Luther.

Satan's plan, of course, is to morally corrupt humanity, so he can separate us from God and starve our spirits. But before starvation finally destroys the appetite, it makes us even more desperate.

Simply Radical

The stars always shine. You can't see them in the daytime, because it's not dark enough. The darker the darkness and the longer you've lived in it, the brighter a light appears to you. For someone who has lived in a totally darkened room for a month, a small light is almost blinding.

Jesus said that we were not to put our light under a bushel basket but on a lamp stand so that all can see. In times of moral and spiritual darkness, it doesn't take much to be a radical Christian and a bright-shining light. Simply believing in God, trusting in Christ for your salvation and living a pure life is so revolutionary to some people, they can scarcely comprehend it. A bold and up-front disciple of Jesus Christ will never have more effect on others than when darkness is everywhere.

There's a lot of sin and depraved thinking around today, but we have good reason to believe that revival is coming. Even as things get worse—hang in there. And remember, the devil will always overplay his hand!

So the light continues to shine in the darkness, for the darkness has never overpowered it. (John 1:5, Williams)

Time 2
REMEMBER GOD'S
GREAT POWER

The children of Israel were told over and over to remember the things that God had done for them and to pass those stories on to their children. The recollections of God's great power and provision not only reminded them of their covenant with God, but also gave them confidence to put their trust in God's power in the midst of darkness.

1. In the following materials, you'll find exciting stories of how God has moved with great power in the midst of dark situations:

> David L. McKenna, *The Coming Great Awakening* (InterVarsity, 1990).
>
> W. A. Pratney, *Revival* (Whitaker House, 1983).
>
> "Awakening in America," *Christian History*, Vol. VIII, no. 3, pp. 22, 27.
>
> Robert E. Coleman, *One Divine Moment* (Fleming H. Revell, 1970).
>
> Corrie Ten Boom, *The Hiding Place* (Barbour, 1991).

2. Start your own *Book of Remembrance* notebook to record your prayers and God's answers. You can also write down testimonies from the lives of friends and family when you hear accounts of God's work in their lives. Not only will this help you organize your prayer life and recognize God's answers to your prayers, but it can also help you make it through tough times.

4

A JUDGMENT DAY IS COMING
(But Someone's Standing in the Gap)

Jump-Starting a Revival

Have you been hoping for revival in your school, your church, your personal life? You need to read this:

On the morning of Tuesday, February 3, 1970, something unexpected happened during a normally uneventful chapel service. Asbury, a small college located in the western Kentucky town of Wilmore, was host to an event that was truly out of this world. On the following evening, the news anchor for WLEX-TV in Lexington, Kentucky, opened the broadcast like this:

Something is taking place at the college campus at
Wilmore which touched me about as much as anything

that has occurred in my thirty-four years of news reporting.

I know normally when you are watching television like everyone else, you have one eye perhaps on the paper and one eye on the television or one ear to someone else in the room or perhaps you are fixing the evening meal. But for the next two-and-one-half minutes I wish you would stop everything you are doing. I think you are going to be impressed.

*It started at ten o'clock yesterday. Chapel was scheduled to end at eleven o'clock yesterday morning. But it didn't end at eleven o'clock last **night**. It didn't end at eleven o'clock **this morning**. In fact, as Jim and I took the air, it was still going on. Let's have a look and a listen. . .*

Imagine a TV news anchor reporting a prayer service at your school! But then this was no ordinary prayer service. The account of what happened at Asbury is best told by Dr. Dennis Kinlaw, the president of Asbury at that time:

The dean of students was scheduled to speak that morning, but instead he gave his testimony. After speaking, he gave the opportunity for students to stand and share what God was doing in their lives.

About five minutes before chapel was scheduled to be over a philosophy professor turned to the dean, who had

68

come down from the podium to sit on the front row, and said, "God is here. If you give an invitation there will be a response."

*The dean gave an invitation—and that started a response that lasted until eight o'clock the following Tuesday morning **a week later**. That was when we began classes again.*[1]

The chapel service went on day and night for several days, propelled by a sense of the presence of God. No preaching took place, but an informal order began to take shape. A student stood and shared how God was dealing with him or her, and others spontaneously came and knelt at the altar. There was prayer followed by singing and praise. Then more people shared how God was cleaning up their lives and straightening out bad relationships.

At night when the long-distance phone rates went down, students lined up at the phones. They eagerly called friends and family to relate what was happening to them. Dr. Kinlaw continues:

What had been tradition became reality. What existed only in religious vocabulary became human experience. The emphasis was never on gifts of the Spirit but on personal sin and reconciliation with God and other people.[2]

When the chapel meeting finally concluded, it had lasted 166 hours. Classes were canceled for the entire week. In the days that followed many students went out to churches and other campuses all over the United States and Canada to testify about the experience they'd had with God. Wherever they went revivals and spiritual awakenings began that lasted sometimes for years. There is no way of knowing the number of people brought into the kingdom of God by the revival fires that began at Asbury.

As one student simply put it, "God came to our campus."

God came . . . Isn't that what *we're* longing for?

Fanning the Flames of Revival

Maybe you've been too busy looking at the dry indifference to God all around you. Maybe you think that conditions are not right for a revival anywhere near you.

Recently, huge fires swept through the canyons of southern California destroying hundreds of homes and burning tens of thousands of acres. This "fire storm," driven by the Santa Ana winds, spread through the underbrush faster than a person could run. Why? Because it was so dry. That's the way revivals often begin—when things get dry enough.

Praying is like fanning the flames of revival. In a place that is spiritually dry, a little spark can become a raging inferno when it is driven by the wind of the Holy Spirit.

What caused the revival at Asbury? "Maybe it was our need," Kinlaw says. "We needed it worse than anyone else around." But the groundwork for the revival was laid long before Tuesday morning chapel. Kinlaw goes on to relate the prayer experiment that preceded the February 3 outpouring:

Some students began to pray. One girl had a great burden for revival at Asbury. So she gathered a group around her and started praying. In October, four months before the Spirit came in February, six students banded together in what they called "the great experiment." They covenanted to spend thirty minutes every morning, for thirty days, in prayer and Bible reading, writing down what truth they got from the Word each day, sharing their faith somewhere in the course of the day. They all met once a week during those thirty days to check up on each other.[3]

That group held several all-night prayer meetings, where they prayed for God to come to the campus. When they finished a prayer meeting, they'd look at each other and ask, "Do you think he'll come today?

At the beginning of the winter term, each of those six students picked out five other students to meet with. So now there were six groups of six getting up and praying for thirty minutes each morning. That experiment ended the 31st of January. On that day those thirty-six students were the ones to lead the chapel service. One after another they shared what God had done for them, and challenged every student on campus to become part of a group of six who would for thirty days engage in this experiment. That was Saturday, January 31. The next chapel was Tuesday, February 3.

The Great Prayer Revival

One of the greatest revivals in American history started as a prayer meeting. The year was 1857. You're probably thinking those were the good old days when *everybody* loved the Lord.

Not hardly.

Yes, there was a great spiritual awakening in the early years of that century. But the spiritual, moral and economic conditions had declined again for years and were at the lowest point since the days preceding that last great revival. J. Edwin Orr, an historian and authority on spiritual awakenings, lists five characteristics of the period. Do any of these sound familiar?

1. materialism, gambling and greed

2. spiritism and the occult

3. immorality

4. commercial and political corruption

5. apathy and indifference to God.[4]

Jeremiah Lamphier, a nineteenth-century New York businessman, was burdened by the tremendous need for God in that city. Lamphier walked the streets, passing out brochures for a noon-day prayer meeting to be held Wednesdays at the Dutch Church in downtown New York. On the first Wednesday he waited alone for thirty minutes. Eventually six men showed up. The next week there were twenty, and by the end of the first week they had decided to meet daily. Within six months, over ten thousand businessmen met daily in similar meetings, confessing sin, getting saved and praying for revival. Churches began to work together, forgetting their doctrinal differences, and in just two years one million converts were added to churches of all denominations. The effects on the moral and spiritual conditions of the country continued for almost half a century. It is called today *The 1857 Prayer Revival.* Others have called it the *Third Great Awakening.*[5]

No wonder students who want to have a prayer meeting in their schools get so much opposition! It's dangerous for the kingdom of darkness.

Maybe it seems like the Holy Spirit is not moving at all in your town or on your campus. Don't be discouraged. Begin to pray! If there's only a little spark, the wind of the Holy Spirit can turn it into a raging revival fire.

The Judge of the Nations

I was at the Lincoln Memorial in Washington, D.C., filming a segment for the music video, *The Standard.* Two of Lincoln's speeches, the *Gettysburg Address* and the *Second Inaugural Address,* are engraved in stone on the inside wall of the building. As I read his words I realized that Abraham Lincoln had a profound understanding of how the tragic events of his lifetime were a result of God's judgment on America. You've got to read this from Lincoln's Second Inaugural Address:

> *If we shall suppose that American slavery is one of those offenses which, in the providence of God, must needs come, but which, having continued through His appointed time, He now wills to remove and that He gives to both North and South this terrible war as the woe due to those by whom the offense came, shall we*

discern therein any departure from those divine attributes which the believers in a living God always ascribe to Him? Fondly do we hope—fervently do we pray—that this mighty scourge of war may speedily pass away. Yet, if God wills that it continue, until all the wealth piled by the bondman's two hundred and fifty years of unrequited toil shall be sunk, and until every drop of blood drawn with the lash, shall be paid by another drawn with the sword, as was said three thousand years ago, so still it must be said "The judgments of the Lord, are true and righteous altogether."

God not only judges individuals, he judges nations as well. Lincoln understood the Civil War as God's judgment on America for tolerating slavery. Since nations as a whole are not granted heaven or sentenced to hell, their judgment must take place on this side of eternity—in this life.

The judgment of God does not come in immediate response to every sin. On the other hand, just because judgment is delayed doesn't mean it will be delayed forever. God sees everything, and he forgets nothing. Unrepentant nations and individuals often store up judgment for themselves as they resist God's efforts to bring them to repentance. Though he extends grace to them giving them more time to turn around, they press on deeper into their sin—only to accumulate more judgment for themselves.

In the parable of the talents, each servant was given a responsibility. Then the master goes away. In several of Jesus' parables the master leaves, only to return suddenly and unexpectedly to see what they have been doing in his absence. Some people go on sinning because they see no signs of God's judgment. They suppose he doesn't care. That, my friend, is a big mistake.

In another parable, a man planted a vineyard, put a wall around it, dug a vat under the wine press and erected a tower. Then he rented it out to vine-growers and went off on a trip. Periodically, the owner sent messengers to collect the profits. But the servants refused to listen to the messenger, and they would not give to the owner what belonged to him. Finally, the owner sent his son. The wicked servants killed the son, thinking the vineyard would then be theirs (Mark 12).

In that parable Jesus referred to the nation of Israel. They had rejected and killed God's prophets in earlier days. In the end they wound up crucifying the Son of God himself. They continued to persecute and kill the followers of Jesus until finally the cup of their iniquity overflowed and judgment came on them swiftly. In his last confrontation with the Jewish high court, the Sanhedrin, Jesus pronounced judgment on them with these words:

> **Fill up, then, the measure of the sin of your forefathers! . . . I am sending you prophets and wise men and teachers. Some of them you will kill and crucify; others you will flog in your synagogues and pursue from town to town. And so upon you will come all the righteous blood that has been shed on**

earth, from the blood of righteous Abel to the blood of Zechariah . . . whom you murdered . . . I tell you the truth, all this will come upon this generation.

O Jerusalem, Jerusalem, you who kill the prophets and stone those sent to you, how often I have longed to gather your children together, as a hen gathers her chicks under her wings, but you were not willing. Look, your house is left to you desolate. (Matt. 23:32-38)

Finally, the cup of their iniquity overflowed when the religious leaders killed James, Jesus' half brother. Josephus, the Jewish historian, recorded the event. James was revered by all the Jews. But he was thrown from the wall of the temple by the religious leaders because he confessed that Christ was the risen Messiah. Immediately after the martyrdom of James, the Roman armies surrounded Jerusalem in 70 A.D. and destroyed it completely. Even the Jews, who had not believed Jesus, considered those dark days to be a judgement of God brought on by the murder of James.[6]

Accounting for National Sins

There's a lot of concern these days about piling up nuclear waste. This stuff doesn't go away. The fear is that the methods of disposing of radioactive material will many years from now come back to haunt us. Sin is like that too. If you don't dispose of it properly, its consequences sooner or later will certainly come back on you with a vengeance.

The United States of America is piling up iniquity as high as the Rockies. In addition to *private sector sins* there are numerous *national sins* for which we will have to answer.

Millions of abortions have been performed in America in the last twenty years. More than four thousand innocent lives are taken each day. This has been made possible by the Supreme Court, in their 1973 *Roe v. Wade* decision.

The United States is the world's leading producer of pornography, and the largest consumer of child pornography.

When Israel neglected to teach the history of God's intervention to their children, the new generation forgot about God and wandered into pagan idolatry. As a nation, it seems we are trying desperately to eliminate from our memory the great things God has done for us.

The youngest and the future generations, more than any other, are the ones being defrauded. Child pornography, abortion, revisionist history that eliminates God, not to mention the enormous national debt we are charging to future generations, are all generational sins. Jesus said this about sins against the youngest and weakest:

> **And whoever welcomes a little child like this in my name welcomes me. But if anyone causes one of these little ones who believe in me to sin, it would be better for him to have a large millstone hung around his neck and to be drowned in the depths of the sea. (Matt. 18:5-6)**

When the Supreme Court decided that indiscriminate massacre of the unborn was acceptable, that prayer in public school was forbidden and that the Ten Commandments should not be displayed on the wall of a school room, it in effect constituted a *formalized rejection* of God. I've heard people question how much good prayer in public schools did or would do again. First of all, prayer is more effective than most people think. Second, throwing it out made the rejection of God formal, legal and official.

It's not only the Supreme Court that has been responsible for a national rejection of God and his law. Bill Clinton was elected president of the United States in 1992, running on a platform that included support for abortion-on-demand and the establishment of homosexuals as a legally protected minority. Whether you agree or disagree with Clinton's economic plan or his foreign policy is beside the point. In the 1992 election we as a nation determined that issues such as historic Christian values, godliness and biblical morality were unimportant. The economy was what really mattered. The 1992 presidential election was a formal statement of our rejection of God's law as the foundation of our national morality.

We still print "In God We Trust" on our coins and currency. Rumors spread about efforts to remove the phrase proved to be unfounded. Nevertheless, don't let anyone tell you that it doesn't matter whether or not our money says "In God We Trust." The spirit of this age and those motivated by it want to remove all reference to God and our dependency on him. It is a spirit that refuses to acknowledge God and proclaims that we have risen as a nation by our own might and wisdom.

The House the Lord Built

For any nation without God, all the social engineering and economic theories are useless. We can have government programs, committees and subcommittees and billion-dollar budgets for every conceivable problem in our world. But the problems are not going away. Rather, they are escalating out of control. People are frustrated with government officials and are demanding that our leaders do something to make things better. Those who look to government and the people who serve in government to solve all their problems need to realize that more government is not the answer. We need God in America again.

At a critical point in their history, Israel decided it didn't want to be a nation under God, a nation that could say, *In God We Trust.* The people wanted a king—someone who would take dictatorial authority, if only he would solve all their problems.

Well, they got their king, but, just as God had warned, it cost them dearly.

When people no longer trust God but instead look to government to meet their needs, they create a civil monster that eventually enslaves them. Big government not only takes away our money, but our children and their freedoms as well. It's time to realize that what the psalmist wrote is true:

Unless the Lord builds the house, its builders labor in vain. Unless the Lord watches over the city, the watchmen stand guard in vain. (Ps. 127:1)

The Constitutional Convention in 1787 was about to give up in its efforts to mold thirteen states into a United States. Benjamin Franklin stood before the divided and disagreeing delegates and called them all to prayer with these words:

> *In the beginning of the contest with Britain, when we were sensible of danger, we had daily prayers in this room for divine protection. Our prayers, sir, were heard; and they were graciously answered . . . I have lived a long time; and the longer I lived the more convincing proofs I see of this truth, that God governs in the affairs of men. And if a sparrow cannot fall to the ground without his notice, is it probable that an empire can rise without his aid? We have been assured, sir, in the sacred writings, that "except the Lord build the house, they labor in vain that build it." I firmly believe this, and I also believe that, without his concurring aid, we shall succeed in this political building no better than the builders of Babel.*[7]

Holding Back the Flood of Evil

Did you ever see a door with a dozen locks on it? That's a lot like the door that holds back the flood of evil in a nation. But in our so-called "free" Western society, many of these restraints have been broken. There are only a few things left that still hold the door closed, keeping evil from bursting in to take complete control. What restrains the unbridled release of evil? The prayers of the saints and the ministry of the Spirit through the body of Christ.

In the song, *America Again,* I felt compelled to write that "America's dead and dying hand is on the threshold of the church." That means the only hope for restraining the forces of evil that will lead us to chaos and a barbaric society is for America to reach inside the doors of our churches where they can hear the Word of God and respond once again.

The early '60s were a turning point in American history. The removal of prayer, Bible reading and the Ten Commandments from public schools, and the decision to legalize abortion were two of the major events that signified the beginning of a deterioration in our society.

Between 1960 and 1980, the number of serious crimes (murders, rapes, robberies, burglaries) increased *332 percent.* Annually, fifty-seven million Americans—one in four—are victims of crime.[8]

One way that judgment comes to a nation is when that nation is given over to a form of lawlessness that causes the disintegration of order. Once-civilized communities begin the descent into savage chaos. We are all horrified by the barbaric nature of inner-city America. We are shocked by kids who have thrown off all restraints, and teenagers who murder with cold-blooded ruthlessness, for no reason at all.

The bookstores are full of new titles about what is happening to our society. We are becoming immoral, valueless, barbaric and lawless. These are the signs of God's restraining grace being lifted.

The question is, Where will it all lead? To judgment and chaos—or to revival and a new spiritual awakening. It may depend on who—*if anyone*—is standing in the gap for our nation.

How Many Righteous in Sodom?

On his way to visit Sodom and Gomorrah, the Lord visited Abram one day.

> **Then the Lord said, "The outcry against Sodom and Gomorrah is so great and their sin so grievous that I will go down and see if what they have done is as bad as the outcry that has reached me. If not, I will know. (Gen. 18:20–21)**

The outcry that the Lord speaks of here is a cry for justice and judgment. When the Lord confronted Cain about his murderous sin the Lord said, **"Your brother's blood cries out to me from the ground" (Gen. 4:10)**.

Apparently, Abraham knew about the conditions in Sodom. He also knew his nephew Lot lived there, and if judgment came, Lot would be right in the middle of it. Abraham answered the Lord with these words:

> **"Will you sweep away the righteous with the wicked? What if there are fifty righteous people in the city? Will you really sweep it away and not spare the place for the sake of the fifty righteous people in it? Far be it from you to do such a thing— to kill the righteous with the wicked, treating the righteous and the wicked alike. Far be it from you! Will not the Judge of all the earth do right?"**
>
> **The Lord said, "If I find fifty righteous people in**

the city of Sodom, I will spare the whole place for their sake." (Gen. 18:23-26)

Abraham continued to bargain with God, "What if the fifty righteous are lacking five?"

"Suppose forty are found there?"

"Suppose thirty are found?"

"Suppose twenty are found?"

In each case the Lord said he would not destroy the city if that number of righteous people could be found.

Finally Abraham said, "May the Lord not be angry, but let me speak just once more. What if only ten can be found there?" He answered, **"For the sake of ten, I will not destroy it" (Gen. 18:32)**.

I have heard people try to estimate the population of Sodom and Gomorrah and calculate the percentage of righteous people required to keep it from judgment and destruction. That misses the point altogether. What if Abraham had gone for five righteous people? Can you imagine God sparing Sodom for the sake of five, ten or even a hundred people who committed to righteousness?

What seemed to be the determining factor was not so much the number of the righteous or even the depth of the sins of the wicked. It really came down to two things:

• the faith and persistence of Abraham who interceded on their behalf, and

• the grace and mercy of the Judge.

If we suppose that God's continued grace and mercy on our nation is based on the fact that a majority of the people are Christians, we have greatly misunderstood God. If God pours out his grace on America to revive our spiritual life and moral virtue, it won't be because fifty-one percent of the people are Christians. That would be like saying that you'll go to heaven if you have more good works than bad works. God's patience, God's forgiveness and God's gift of repentance and revival are given by his grace. We never have deserved them and never will. We pray for that revival and the outpouring of the Holy Spirit instead of the judgment we actually deserve.

God has always been gracious to the humble. The apostle James wrote:

But he gives us more grace. That is why Scripture says: "God opposes the proud but gives grace to the humble." (James 4:6)

Our nation is teetering between judgment and mercy. In our government, our schools and the media, God is not acknowledged. People puff themselves up with pride and are arrogant toward God. Consequently, God removes the restraining grace from our nation and things begin to come unglued. We are sinking into moral and ethical confusion, educational and social chaos, lawlessness and economic decline.

Christians must humble themselves and pray for an outpouring of God's mercy and grace:

God, we've sinned as a nation. Our transgressions are piled as high as the mountains, and our cup of iniquity is all but overflowing. But, God, remember your mercy. Send revival instead of the judgment we so greatly deserve.

Someone to Stand in the Gap

Ezekiel prophesied to Israel about coming judgment. For the most part, he was ignored. Finally, Nebuchadnezzar's armies came and took the ten tribes that made up Israel (Judah consisted of the tribes of Benjamin and Judah) captive, dispersed them among the pagan nations, and they were never heard from again. Only the tribes of Benjamin and Judah survived to return to their homeland after seventy years of captivity.

I looked for a man among them who would build up the wall and stand before me in the gap on behalf of the land so I would not have to destroy it, but I found none. So I will pour out my wrath on them and consume them with my fiery anger, bringing down on their own heads all they have done, declares the Sovereign Lord. (Ezek. 22:30-31)

On two occasions the Lord started to bring a final judgment on Israel while they were still in the wilderness. In both cases judgment was averted because there was someone to intercede with the Lord.

While Moses was on Mount Sinai receiving the Ten Commandments, the people built a golden calf and began to worship it. The anger of the Lord burned against them, and he said to Moses:

> **I have seen these people . . . and they are a stiff-necked people. Now leave me alone so that my anger may burn against them and that I may destroy them. Then I will make you into a great nation. (Exod. 32:9-10)**

Moses interceded with God on behalf of the people, reminding him of his promises to Abraham. He prayed that God would glorify himself by extending his mercy. In the end it says:

> **Then the Lord relented and did not bring on his people the disaster he had threatened. (Exod. 32:14)**

There were several occasions that provoked the wrath and judgment of God. Each time Moses interceded for the people and judgment was averted.

At one point, God said to Moses and Aaron, **"Get away from this assembly so I can put an end to them at once"** (**Num. 16:45**). Rather than step back and let judgment come, Moses and Aaron took action.

> **Then Moses said to Aaron, "Take your censer and put incense in it, along with fire from the altar, and**

86

hurry to the assembly to make atonement for them. Wrath has come out from the Lord; the plague has started." So Aaron did as Moses said, and ran into the midst of the assembly. The plague had already started among the people, but Aaron offered the incense and made atonement for them. He stood between the living and the dead, and the plague stopped. (Num. 16:46-48)

God is looking for believers of all ages who will faithfully stand in the gap between a sinful nation and a God of justice to pray for his mercy. Those who intercede for their schools, their communities and their nation not only extend the time given for them to repent, but summon the outpouring of grace and forgiveness that must be present for a nation to turn back to God.

Time 2
MAKE IT HAPPEN

If you are not involved in a prayer group that intercedes for the people you know and the places you live, work or go to school—then take action.

1. If there is no prayer group, start one. Get together to pray before school or work, or at the lunch break. Get together with a Christian friend and do a prayerwalk around your neighborhood and your local high school.

2. Engage yourself in "The Great Experiment," like those students at Asbury. Commit yourself together with five other people for thirty people to pray, read the Bible, share with others and record what God is saying and doing in your lives.

3. Cover your neighborhood, your school, your youth group and your friends with prayer. Pray for God's grace to be extended to our nation and to individuals around you. Pray that the Holy Spirit will convict people of their sin and that he will supply boldness to all the believers to share the Word.

PRAY FOR REVIVAL!

Be bold in your faith to ask for miracles in people's lives. Ask and expect the Holy Spirit to move.

4. Check out these great books on prayer at your local Christian bookstore:

Andrew Murray, *The Believer's School of Prayer* (Bethany House, 1982).

Andrew Murray and Charles Spurgeon, *The Believer's Secret of Intercession* (Bethany House, 1988).

John Dawson, *Taking Your Cities for God* (Creation House, 1989).

Steve Hawthorne and Graham Kendrick, *Prayerwalking* (Creation House, 1993).

Richard Foster, *Prayer* (HarperCollins, 1992).

Peter Lord, *Hearing God* (Baker Book House, 1988).

Patrick Johnstone, *Operation World* (Zondervan, 1993).

Patrick Johnstone, *You Can Change Your World* (for children) (Zondervan, 1993).

5

CHRONOLOGICAL SNOBBERY
(When Everything Old Is Bad)

That Old-Time Religion

Today, it's not just a question of whether that old-time religion is good enough for me. It goes beyond our personal experience—the love, joy and peace we feel.

The question we need to settle in our hearts is this: *Is Christianity the truth?*

For generations in America, the foundational principles of Christianity were accepted as fact. The issue of religion was, for the most part, a matter of living by what everyone believed about God. Up until recently, the common sin was *Christian backsliding.* Today, it is atheism and paganism. Unbelief used to mean not trusting Jesus Christ as much as you should. Now it means rejecting the notion of the universe as a creation, the Bible as God's Word, the cross as atonement for sin, or right and wrong as moral law. Belief for many comes down to the question of whether God actually exists.

Why is this question so urgent? Because if there is no God then there is no moral law—and then *anything* goes.

Defending your faith is not something that happens only on college campuses. The attack on Christian principles begins much earlier. Cartoons, textbooks, movies, rock and pop music, so-called "family-oriented" sitcoms and anti-Christian teachers—all launch a constant barrage of assaults against Christian beliefs.

Chronological Snobbery

Most of the phrases used to discredit the Bible and intimidate Christians fall into the *you're-just-old-fashioned* category. Are ideas wrong simply because they're old? They are if you listen to the priests and prophets of today's new cultural religion—progressive paganism.

Peter Kreeft's book, *Between Heaven and Hell*, is a fictional dialog between C. S. Lewis, John F. Kennedy and the philosopher Aldous Huxley. Strangely, all three of these men died on November 22, 1963. In Kreeft's little book, the three men meet and, realizing that they have all just died, begin to debate what will happen next to them. Lewis represents the Christian viewpoint, Kennedy the modern humanist viewpoint, and Huxley the eastern pantheist viewpoint.

In this passage, Lewis and Kennedy talk about whether some of Kennedy's ideas should be called heretical.

> *Kennedy:* I still wish we could avoid that label
>   (heresy).

Lewis: Why?

Kennedy: It's . . . so . . . so outdated. So unenlightened. So medieval. So primitive.

Lewis: Jack, do you tell time with an argument?

Kennedy: What?

Lewis: I said, do you tell time with an argument?

Kennedy: What in the world do you mean by that?

Lewis: When you want to know what time it is, what do you look at? An argument or a clock?

Kennedy: A clock, of course.

Lewis: And what do you use an argument for, if not to tell time?

Kennedy: Why, to prove something, of course. Or to try to.

Lewis: So you tell time by the clock and truth by an argument.

Kennedy: Among other means, yes.

Lewis: Not vice versa?

Kennedy: No.

Lewis: But you were trying to tell truth by the clock a minute ago.

Kennedy: Truth by the clock?

Lewis: When I want to disprove an idea, I try to prove that it is *false*. *Your* argument against my idea that your belief was a heresy was simply that my idea was *old*. *Outdated*, I believe you said. *Medieval* and *primitive* were two more of your terms. Those are all clock words, or calendar words. (Calendars are only big, long clocks, after all).[1]

Chronological snobbery is the attempt to discredit or disprove an idea merely by dating it, usually dating it as very old.[2]

We live in a world that assumes that everything new is *progressive* and *enlightened,* while everything old or traditional is bad. Not only is old truth bad, we are told, but those who believe and hold on to such old things are considered the cause of all the world's problems. Consequently, Christians eventually are blamed for everything. But it is ironic that those who call us *old-fashioned* are the ones who themselves are outdated and intellectually off-track.

Where does this chronological snobbery come from? It starts with one of the fundamentals of our new way of thinking.

"The New Monkeys Are Always Smarter"

Evolutionary theory as it has been taught in public schools over the last thirty years has had a profound effect on the way we think.

According to Charles Darwin's theory, organisms are always getting stronger and smarter through the process of natural selection. The weaker members of a species die away, and those that are naturally selected, because of their stronger characteristics, live to pass on their genes to future generations. In this way of thinking, the newer generation that survives is always superior to the older generation. What is new is good, and what is old is inferior and doomed to pass away.

94

According to evolutionary theory, the human race also is bettering itself. Through this process of natural selection, we are supposedly climbing to higher levels, both mentally and physically. New ideas and new ways of living are simply the next stage of our "evolutionary development." Old beliefs and traditional values are part of an inferior age that is being replaced by the evolutionary progress of humanity. Holding on to old beliefs (like Christianity) and old values (like the Ten Commandments) only hinders our progress to a greater human race and a greater society.

Wrong.

Hasn't it occurred to these people that the farther away we get from a Christian-based society, the more chaotic and barbaric our culture becomes, and the more dictatorial the government grows? If it has dawned on them, they're not telling. They forge ahead, thinking they're creating a "brave new world."

But a world based on an evolutionary values system is animalistic. The only virtue is to survive. If people are in need — well, they're just weak. The natural process will eliminate them.

The concept of right and wrong becomes a religious myth. The only value that matters is self-interest. Everything of the past—religion, traditional value, cultural standard—is outdated and will be left behind in the wake of evolutionary progress. In other words, *old is bad.*

Another Bad Idea

The theory of evolution came along at the right time for another idea: Marxism.

Karl Marx believed there was a force throughout history that causes societies to evolve into the perfect state—a completely communist state. The theory is called *dialectic materialism.* Through the process of unrest and conflict, each new state that emerges from revolution is thought to be closer to an *ideal*, perfect state. The goal is always to tear down the old, the existing or the traditional so that something new might emerge—whatever it may be. There will be one king of kings and lord of lords—the communist state, where there is no private property and no belief in God. Morality is based only on what is good for the state. If you live in a country like this, your value depends on how much you are worth to the state. In one sense, you're like a farmer's prized pig at a county fair: As long as you keep winning you're fine. When you get too old . . . well, it's sausage city.

But Karl Marx had a few things wrong. *Jesus* is the King of Kings and the Lord of Lords. And history is not guided by the plots of murderous revolutionaries. History is guided by the Father's plan, and we find meaning and purpose as we are used by him to bring more light, life and love into this world.

The communist system has proven itself to be a disaster. Yet in America, you'd think we were trying to model our future after the Soviet Union. When a society rejects the Bible and God as Lord and Creator, they inevitably start down the same road the Soviets traveled. It is like we're passing the refugees who are fleeing from the ruins of a collapsed city, and eagerly hurrying to take up residence in their ruined homes!

Don't Confuse Me With the Facts

The philosophy of the present age is based on a few principles, all of which are strongly opposed to Christianity. But most of the opposition is based on false assumptions that our opponents do not like to talk about, even among themselves.

For instance, evolution is accepted and taught as proven, established fact. No question about its validity, right?

Wrong!

It is only theory, and unproven at that. For evolution to be considered scientific fact, all the evidence should substantiate the theory. But does it?

The Wall Street Journal reported that in the Fall of 1993, Dean Kenyon, biology professor at San Francisco State University, was ordered by John Hafernik, chairman of the department, to stop teaching creationism in his introductory biology class.

Professor Kenyon, a distinguished author and authority on chemical evolutionary theory, wasn't exactly teaching creationism. He merely told his students that current evolutionary theory raised philosophical questions and that living systems displayed evidence of intelligent design.

When Kenyon asked for clarification on the order from the dean, he was told it was "forbidden to mention to students that there are important disputes among scientists about whether or not chemical evolution could have taken place on the ancient earth."

Kenyon insisted that he did teach the dominant scientific view of evolution but that he also discussed problems with that view and what some biologists see as evidence of intelligent design. As a result, Dr. Kenyon was yanked from teaching introductory biology and reassigned to labs.

Both the San Francisco State University's Academic Freedom

Committee and the American Association of University Professors insist that Dr. Kenyon's academic freedom has beeen violated and insist the situation be rectified. At the time *The Wall Street Journal*'s article was published, the chairman of the biology department had continued to emphatically reject their recommendations.[3]

Scientists who are also Christians believe that species adapt to their environment—but they observe that genetic changes that occur are not great enough to cause one species to become another. Evolutionary scientists finally are admitting that the fossil record does not support the idea of a gradual change from one animal to another. But since they cannot believe a supernatural creation is possible, they developed yet another theory.

Now we have *macro evolution*. According to this theory, one species suddenly turns into another. How does that happen? To be honest, they have no evidence—but the only other theory available is creationism, which is unacceptable to them.

Although there is evidence that points to a creation, scientists often *start* with the assumption that creation *could not* have happen. Therefore, they must develop some other theory to explain the data.

Taking the Leap of Doubt

The theory of evolution is not only unproven, it's full of problems. Marxism, a colossal failure as an economic and cultural system, has never worked anywhere. Yet, both evolution and Marxism still are taught in schools and even serve as the foundation for modern thinking.

Some evolutionists react with smugness to anyone who believes in a divine creation, a result of their starting with the assumption that there is no God. Creation *could not* have happened because they *know* there is no Creator.

According to Proverbs 14:1, a fool says in his heart that there is no God. Why is it foolish to say there is no God? Because you can't prove it. You can't prove something does not exist, unless you happen to know everything.

Critics of the Bible commit the same logical errors. They begin with assumptions that prevent them from arriving at obvious conclusions. Some of these scholarly critics go to great lengths to conclude that none of the miracles of the New Testament occurred. They claim that Jesus' miracles were fabricated and have no basis in truth, and that the gospel stories were created by the Church over a hundred years after the birth of Christianity.

But their argument is flawed, because they start with this incorrect assumption: *Miracles do not happen because they cannot happen.* From there, these scholars set out to find another explanation for the miracles reported in the Gospels. Ignoring eyewitness accounts and other evidence for believing the Gospels are true, they arrive at their far-fetched conclusions.

Their reasonings and their conclusions make sense, *if* you agree with their starting point—that miracles do not happen. But if you believe that miracles may happen, then you come to a quite different conclusion.

It is ironic that evolution and today's biblical criticism—the prime reasons given for rejecting Christianity—are both based on great leaps of *doubt.* At the same time, the beliefs of Christians routinely are rejected simply because they are old ideas.

The Real Problem With Creation

What's the big deal about creation? Why is it so hard to accept that God is the Creator? It's not a question of evidence, because many people reject creation before they even look at the evidence. For them, creation *did not* happen because it *cannot* happen, and it cannot happen because there is no Creator. That's their starting point.

The implications of divine creation cause skeptics to reject it right off the bat. If there is a creation, then there has to be a Creator—that's what is so difficult for them to accept. But as scientists uncover the complexities of life and the universe, evidence grows stronger that our world did *not* happen by accident, but was put together by design.

The origin of humanity and the universe is not so much a scientific question as it is a question of moral accountability. In 1828, Noah Webster wrote in his first dictionary, "The labor of making or producing any thing constitutes one of the highest and most indefensible titles to property."[4] If God created us, then we belong to him. We are God's property, not our own.

That idea is so repugnant to those whose thinking is bitten by the spirit of this age that they reject it straightaway. Suggest that you are God's property and that he has the right to be your Lord, and you'll most likely get a negative and sometimes angry reaction. People's passionate responses show that you have touched the root issue.

In a way, God owns us twice. Not only has he created us, but when he saw that we were enslaved by the power of the enemy, he set out to redeem us by his blood. In antiquity, conquering armies commonly carried back conquered peoples to their nations as captives. Some became slaves, while those with wealthy and influential friends were held hostage until they were redeemed with the price of a ransom. Similarly, when we were captured by the power of sin and Satan, God redeemed his own possession with the precious blood of Christ.

If we are God's special creation, then we are accountable to him as Lord and Creator.

Consenting Sinners

How many times have you heard people say:

•"Premarital sex isn't wrong—not if we really love each other."

•"Homosexuality is all right. It's your choice—as long as it's between consenting adults."

•"Why is taking drugs wrong if it doesn't hurt anyone else?"

It's not only an issue of hurting someone else. It's a matter of violating and distorting God's creation. When we sin against our bodies or violate our spirits, we sin against God's property.

> **Flee from sexual immorality. All other sins a man commits are outside his body, but he who sins sexually sins against his own body. Do you not know that your body is a temple of the Holy Spirit, who is in you, whom you have received from God? You are**

not your own; you were bought at a price. Therefore honor God with your body. (1 Cor. 6:18-20)

God owns us as if we were property—but he exalts us as if we were kings. He is our Judge, not because he is bigger, but because he is better and because he is our Creator. We will account for everything he entrusted to us—including our lives and our bodies.

If we are here by accident then there is no reason we should give honor, glory or obedience to God. But if we are his creation put here at his will, then he has the right to be King of Kings and Lord of Lords.

Blinded Eyes and Twisted Hearts

Jesus went into the temple and preached to the Jews:

If anyone chooses to do God's will, he will find out whether my teaching comes from God or whether I speak on my own. (John 7:17)

Jesus put his finger on their problem. It wasn't that they did not know what the Scriptures said. It was not an intellectual problem that kept them from believing or perceiving the truth, which was staring them in the face. They did not understand because of the evil in their hearts.

People make a lot of excuses for not accepting Jesus Christ as their Lord and Savior:

•"What about evolution?"

•"The church is full of hypocrites."

•"How do you know the Bible hasn't been changed through all the years?"

Have they investigated the matter thoroughly and come to intellectual conclusions about the reasonableness of Christianity? That is almost never the case. The problem is usually in their hearts, not in their heads. Most objections you hear are people merely parroting things they have heard others say.

Ask them: "If you knew that the world was created by God, if you knew the Bible we have today is a true and accurate record of what happened, and if you knew that Jesus Christ actually rose from the dead—if you knew that all of this was true, would you give your life to Christ and become his disciple?"

Many times the answer is no. Why? Because those objections are not the real obstacle. The problem all along is that their heart is *addicted* to sin and self, and they *do not want* to serve God. Their opposition to Christianity is not intellectual. They simply do not want Christ to reign over them!

It is the same with many intellectual opponents who don't want to accept creation, the resurrection or the truth of the Bible. These things run contrary to their moral, personal or political agendas.

Again, listen to Peter Kreeft's fictional dialog between C. S. Lewis and John F. Kennedy. Lewis has pressed the issue about the evidence of Christ's resurrection and the logical reasons to believe that Jesus was God come in the flesh. Kennedy can't refute the argument, but doesn't want to accept the conclusion.

Lewis: I practiced just the sort of self-deceptive rationalization I've warned you about for many years. I hated the thought of a God who literally barged into our world and our species, who interfered with our lives and our values and perhaps even our human nature. I hated it because I wanted to be on my own, to be my own boss, my own God. And I'm convinced that many people reject Christianity—traditional, biblical, orthodox Christianity, with its active, loving, interfering, demanding God—for that reason. Not because the evidence proves it's untrue, but because they don't want it to be true.

Dusting Off the Cobwebs of Paganism

Critics try to browbeat Christians with the fact that their beliefs and values are old. Actually, the opposite is true. Those who conveniently go along and accept the philosophy and values of this present age are the ones who are old-fashioned. The New Age movement is nothing more than ancient, pagan occultism. Those who have a *if-it-feels-good-do-it* approach to life resurrect an old, fourth century B.C. philosophy called Epicurianism. The Epicurian philosophers, whose basic beliefs were running from pain and living for pleasure, were challenged by Paul in a confrontation at Mars Hill (Acts 17).

Worn-out socialism, ancient mysticism and Greek Epicurianism—these are the philosophies that kept the world in darkness economically, politically and culturally. It was only by the spread of the gospel and the Bible that we came to understand the value of the individual. Each person has worth because of the value God places on us. Only because of the spread of the gospel was scientific revolution made possible. It is Christianity that has brought people out of barbarism and darkness into light. But the farther away we move from Christianity, the more we lose those ideals.

Christianity has been the light of the world. The philosophy that undergirds this present age signals a retreat into paganism and into a new Dark Age. Christianity has fostered music, the arts, education and literature. Those who reject Christianity often are in the business of turning those disciplines into perverted expression of humanity's sin nature.

Don't let anyone tell you that you are old-fashioned. Committed Christians are those who stand in the truth. They are the *enlightened* ones in the midst of a multitude that is marching our world back into darkness. But it doesn't have to be that way. Christians need to put their light on a hilltop and let it shine.

We are not old-fashioned. What we believe is the light of the world, and the hope of humanity.

Time 2
MAKE IT HAPPEN

It's not enough to get excited and feel good about being a Christian. You need to understand why Christianity is the truth. Here are some suggestions:

Things To Read

Josh McDowell, *Evidence That Demands A Verdict, Vols. 1 and 2* (Thomas Nelson, 1992). These two books are a great source for reports and debates. They are written in an outline format with all the arguments, sources and quotes you'll ever need.

The Evolution Conspiracy (video) (Jeremiah Films, 1989).

John Stott, *Basic Christianity* (InterVarsity, 1979).

Peter Kreeft, *Between Heaven & Hell* (InterVarsity, 1982). Other great books by Peter Kreeft include *The Unaborted Socrates* (InterVarsity, 1983) and *Socrates Meets Jesus* (InterVarsity, 1987).

Things To Do

1. Have a *Creation versus Evolution* debate in your school. This is perfectly legal if it is sponsored by a Bible Club or some other student group and students are not forced to attend. If school administrators hesitate because of a separation-of-church-and-state concern, remind them that the Supreme Court ruled in *Mergens v. Westside Community Board of Education* that Bible Clubs can hold, sponsor and advertise meetings like any other club. Even though the content of those meetings is religious, it does not constitute a violation of the first amendment.

If you are denied the freedoms of other student groups, politely and non-threateningly remind administrators of the *Mergens* decision. If, however, school administrators are determined to deny you equal access to school facilities, contact:

The American Center for Law and Justice
P.O. Box 64429
Virginia Beach, VA 23467
(phone) 804/523-7570

2. *Faith With Reason*, one of our own *Time 2* videos, can be shown at activity period, sponsored by your Bible Club, or at an informal gathering. My guest in the video is Josh McDowell. Order this video by contacting Carman Ministries, P.O. Box 701050, Tulsa, OK 74170, or call 1-800/79TIME2.

THERE ARE A LOT OF GREAT THINGS IN LIFE FOR YOU
(But the Enemy of the Best Is the Good)

If You Can't Win, Change the Rules

How do you know if an object is one meter long? What if it's important to know the measurement exactly? Fortunately, there are people who care about precision! Just listen to this.

In 1889, the International Bureau of Weights and Measures established the international prototype meter. They put two marks on a stick, actually a bar of ninety percent platinum and ten percent iridium, and made that distance the standard by which all meter sticks would be calibrated. Those two marks were supposed to be a simpler way of *standardizing* the meter. Before that, the meter was defined by the French Academy of Sciences as *1/10,000,000 of the quadrant of the Earth's circumference running from the North Pole through Paris to the equator.* In 1960, the standard became even more exact: *1,650,763.73 wavelengths of light in a vacuum, of the orange-red line in the spectrum of the krypton-86 atom.* Now, a true meter is defined as *the distance traveled by light in a vacuum in 1/299,792,458 of a second.*[1]

Science and technology are becoming more exacting in the way they measure their standards. Pretty strange, isn't it, that at the same time, the rest of the world is casting off its social, moral and educational standards.

The length of a meter is absolute and does not change. You can't arbitrarily cut off a couple of centimeters from your meter stick if it suits your purposes. A meter stick is only good if it measures up to the standard.

The measurements of weights have equally exacting standards. One of the oldest forms of thievery is "shaving the weights." It used to be that merchants measured grain by using weights and counterbalances. Customers who thought they were getting a pound of grain would be cheated because the one-pound counterweight had been shaved down so that it weighed less than a pound.

Because the Lord hated the kind of evil heart that would defraud someone, Proverbs 11:1 says: **"The Lord abhors dishonest scales, but accurate weights are his delight."** One of the characteristics of our generation is that people want to shave the weights and lower the standards.

God and his Word are the absolute and unchangeable standard of right and wrong. When you take God out of the equation of life, it affects a lot more than your Sunday mornings. *Everything* changes. Eventually, you come to believe that there is no right and wrong.

A 1988 Department of Education book regarding drug curriculum, *Drug Prevention Curricula: A Guide to Selection and Implementation*, summarizes the fundamental components to be included in any drug education program. It gave plenty of information on how to identify drugs and the detrimental effect they have on your body. But one word conspicuously was missing. Nowhere was there any indication that it was *wrong* to take drugs. Without religious foundation, concepts of right and wrong are all relative. So nothing is actually *wrong.*[2]

Now, Let's All Be Equal

You see, if you lower the standards enough, *everyone* will pass the morality test! Nothing is good, nothing is bad. We are all equal, and we are free to do whatever we want ("as long as we don't hurt anyone . . . ").

But God says there *is* right and wrong. He is Judge, and on the last day he will separate the righteous from the wicked. He is the one who weighs nations in the balance. The king of Babylon saw God's handwriting on the wall, and it said, **"You have been weighed on the scales and found wanting" (Dan. 5:27)**.

The greatest sin, according to the humanistic morality of this generation, is to put someone down. "Don't make anyone feel bad. Don't impose your standards on other people. You shouldn't judge others regardless of how lazy they are, how inadequately they perform, or how perverted they have become."

The truth is, sin is making our world crazy. The philosophy of this age not only opposes the Bible, but it's absurd! Standards are continually lowered or even eliminated so that no one will feel bad about failing.

For the last five years many school districts in the United States have redesigned their curriculums around an educational philosophy called Outcome-Based Education (OBE). Its promoters believe that we should make everyone "succeed"—by eliminating grades and standards of performance. In other words, we don't want to make anyone feel bad by flunking them! By the way, none of our Western world counterparts use this method, and they are far ahead of us in education. Strong curriculum in the classroom and graded evaluations have put them in the lead.[3]

Our students scored last in math and science compared to students of other industrialized nations. A 1989 international comparison of mathematics and science skills showed American students scoring at the bottom and South Korean students scoring at the top. South Korean students performed at high levels in math at four times the rate of U.S. students. Ironically, when asked if they are good at math, sixty-eight percent of American students thought they were. That was the highest percentage of any nation.[4]

Our standards in America are constantly being changed in order to put a nice face on mediocrity or even out-and-out failure. Many people are demanding the SAT test be changed in order to bring test scores back up. All we have to do to *look* better is lower the standards some more.

The problem is not just standards for students, but standards for teachers. Twenty-six states require only minimum standards on a competency test. Forty-seven correct answers out of one hundred is considered a passing grade.

In California, thirty-one percent of new teachers failed the state's Basic Education Skills test. Maybe the failure rate is so high because these tests are too hard. Not hardly. The California Teachers Association said, "Any competent high-school student should be able to pass." It is little wonder that the educational establishments resist standards that would hold them or their students accountable.[5]

Funny, but it doesn't work that way. Suppose you could only make 6-feet 3-inches in a high-jump competition. Do you think you could say, "Let's call that seven feet, because I'm a nice guy," and the other competitors would agree?

No, people tend to rise to standards, challenges and expectations, whatever they are. When there are no absolute moral standards, people tend toward absolutely no morality. When anything can pass as good enough, people no longer excel. They "dumb down" to meet the lowered standard.

The Good and Acceptable Standard

Unfortunately, this kind of low-level thinking is carried over by believers into their relationship with God. Too often we think, "What's the minimum I have to do to get by?" Paul wrote to the Romans:

Therefore, I urge you, brothers, in view of God's mercy, to offer your bodies as living sacrifices, holy and pleasing to God—this is your spiritual act of worship. Do not conform any longer to the pattern of

this world, but be transformed by the renewing of your mind. Then you will be able to test and approve what God's will is—his *good, pleasing and perfect will.* (Rom. 12:1-2)

You need to aim for the will of God, which is good, pleasing and perfect. If you get used to standards that float *according to what suits the moment*, you'll be tempted to give up when being a disciple of Jesus Christ becomes challenging.

Romans 12:1 does not say—as some claim—that there are three wills of God. It's not like buying a tire for your car and selecting from one of three options: good, better or best. God's will for your life is good, pleasing *and* perfect—all three. And then there are those who talk about making Jesus their Savior but not the Lord of the lives.

Minimum-standard-seeking is a problem for the church just as it is for the rest of the world. We can't fool anyone but ourselves. Jesus sees the depth of our hearts and motives and knows us better than we know ourselves. Those who are striving for the lowest calling may in the end be unhappily surprised. What if our *savior-not-lord* category doesn't exist?

The Cost of Discipleship

What do you think about the heart of a person who seeks for the least they can do to get by? Have you ever noticed that Jesus responded in different ways regarding the call and cost of discipleship? To the rich young ruler, Jesus said go and sell everything in order to be a disciple (Mark 10:21). To the woman caught in adultery, Jesus simply said, **"Then neither do I condemn you, go now and leave your life of sin" (John 8:11)**. To some he said they were to only believe, to others they had to forsake mother, father, family and self.

At first that may not seem fair or even consistent. But Jesus knew the hearts of those with whom he spoke. When someone's motive was to negotiate the lowest possible standard of discipleship, Jesus always raised it—often beyond what they would bargain for! To those whose heart was to love and follow him, his yoke was easy and his burden was light.

A woman who was a sinner sneaked into a Pharisee's house, and washed Jesus' feet with her tears. Jesus said of her, **"Therefore, I tell you, her many sins have been forgiven—for she loved much . . . " Jesus said to the woman, "Your faith has saved you; go in peace" (Luke 7:47, 50)**.

To be his disciple means that our heart follows after him. When you aim for the lowest level, it shows that even though you may do a lot of good things, your heart is headed in the wrong direction.

Don't just aim for the "acceptable" or "permissive" will of God—as if such a thing even exists. *Go for the high calling*. Seek God's perfect will, the expression of God's purpose in your life. Paul said, **"I press on toward the goal to win the prize for which God has called me heavenward in Christ Jesus" (Phil. 3:14)**.

The Anatomy of Compromise

God called Abraham to leave Ur of the Chaldees and set out for a promised land. So Abraham left with his wife and all that belonged to him. He also took Lot, his brother's son.

God blessed Abraham and Lot so much so that the land could not sustain the flocks and herds of them both. Because of trouble between their herdsmen, Abraham said to his nephew:

"Is not the whole land before you? Let's part company. If you go to the left, I'll go to the right; if you go to the right, I'll go to the left." Lot looked up and saw that the whole plain of the Jordan was well watered, like the garden of the Lord ...
(Gen. 13:9–10)

Lot chose for himself the beautiful valley of the Jordan and took off eastward. His story illustrates three major principles in the progression of compromise:

1. *Compromise begins when you make a decision against the life of faith.*

God had promised Abraham that he would give him a great inheritance. Abraham might have depended on Lot to help him build his flocks, his wealth and his sheep ranch. Instead, he trusted God as his source, and was willing to send away a man who might have helped him become prosperous.

One of my greatest challenges in the walk of faith was God's direction to me to make all my concerts free. No tickets were to be sold and only a love offering was to be taken.

That was hard. Selling tickets is the normal way of meeting expenses, so with that decision, we ventured into uncharted territory.

We have found that having free concerts increases attendance about twenty percent. But the number of people who respond to the altar calls has *doubled*. That was what was on God's heart.

Our method still doesn't work financially. It's rare that the offering covers our expenses. But God always covers them from other sources. There is no specific formula to make it work. It's simply a step of faith, and God always sees to it that something else happens to cover our needs.

The decision to do free concerts carved a path and set me firmly in one direction. On the other hand, once you start down the road to compromise, it becomes increasing difficult to turn back or to walk in faith.

The second principle of compromise is this:

2. *Compromise comes by inches.*

So Lot chose for himself the whole plain of the Jordan and set out toward the east. The two men parted company: Abram lived in the land of Canaan, while Lot lived among the cities of the plain and pitched his tents near Sodom. Now the men of Sodom were wicked and were sinning greatly against the Lord. (Gen. 13:11-13)

First, Lot chose the valley of Sodom. Then he pitched his tents near Sodom. Before long, Lot had his whole family living right in the city. When people turn away from God's highest call for their lives—when they decide against the life of faith, they set off in another direction. Things may work out well in the beginning—they don't completely backslide the next day. But as time goes by, inch by inch, they're moving toward the city. One day, they wake up and realize they're living in Sodom.

Sodom is not a great place to live. Its people have thrown off all restraints, to the point that their sin begs for God's judgment.

That leads to the third principle:

3. *Compromise ends in destruction.*

Second Peter 2:8 says that Lot **"was tormented in his righteous soul by the lawless deeds he saw and heard . . . "** Whatever you compromise to keep, you'll probably wind up losing. Read about Lot if you want to see a man who compromised and lost all he had.

A Momentary Compromise

A couple of months after I became a Christian, my church in Orange, California, had an evangelistic outreach in conjunction with the town's annual street fair. The church was one block from the center of town. They closed off a block in each direction of the town square and had booths with international foods and crafts. In front of the church we had a flat-bed truck outfitted as a concert stage. As people came down, we opened up the doors of the church to let them go inside and watch a free movie. After they came into the church we preached the gospel.

I was the main attraction on the flat-bed truck, and I had to go out and sing secular music. It was the first time as a Christian that I had to do that. Before I was saved I spent a lot of time singing in bars. When I became a Christian, the Holy Spirit dealt with me about it. There was no promise of any other music career in the future. But I knew God wanted me to get out of what I was doing.

The town officials wouldn't allow Christian music at the street fair. The church people told me to sing whatever would draw the people to our end of the street. Based on that I said okay, but I was troubled because I had told the Lord I was through with that type of music. But that day, I wavered in my convictions and sang my secular songs.

We definitely got a crowd, but when it was over I felt terrible. When they started screaming for me, I sensed something I had never felt before. I realized that God is the one who should receive this glory. I had never understood that before, because I didn't have the Lord in me.

I decided that day that I was finished with secular music, and that I would not compromise concerning what God had told me to do. I determined to be bold and up-front about Jesus Christ.

Years later, record company executives finally realized that my commitment to boldly proclaim the name of Jesus Christ in everything I did was not negotiable. I was never going to cross over to secular music for them. Whether I produce platinum records and pack arenas, or I only sing in small country churches, Jesus Christ will be proclaimed boldly in my music.

Since then, we have negotiated a recording contract with The Sparrow Corporation that is putting our albums in every major secular store in the country—without compromising God's directions to me, and without veiling the message. If you follow

God faithfully without compromise, he will open every door you need to walk through.

The Power of Influence

Years later God told Abraham that he would not destroy the city if he could find ten righteous men (Gen. 18:32). That doesn't sound too difficult, does it? But after all that time living in Sodom, Lot had not won over even ten men! One of the effects of compromise is that our words have no power. When Lot finally tried to take a stand and warn his children about the impending judgment, even they would not listen. **"But his sons-in-law thought he was joking" (Gen. 19:14)**.

When you live what you preach, it puts power in your words. But no one takes a compromiser seriously. As I said, before I became a Christian I sang in bars. People in bars are always talking about supernatural things—things that go bump in the night. They'll even discuss being born-again, going to heaven or hell and how they need to stop sinning. But there's no power in their words, because they don't live by what they are saying.

The power of your words to influence people around you is determined partially by the sincerity of your faith. Don't talk the talk if you don't walk the walk. They won't listen.

But aren't we supposed to be in the world as a witness? Yes, *in* the world, not *of* it. Jesus himself was a friend of sinners. But you can't compromise your faith in Christ in order to be accepted by the world. If you do, your witness will have no power to change lives. I greatly desire to reach out to those who live in Sodom, but I'll never hide my commitment to Christ to do it.

The Enemy of the Best . . .

The enemy of God's best is usually some good thing that you do in place of God's perfect plan for you. Mary came to Jesus, broke the alabaster box filled with expensive perfumed oil and used it to anoint him. Judas said, "Why this waste? It could have been sold and given to the poor." Judas's point was this: *Do something good with your best—but don't waste it on Jesus.*

But if you are going to follow Jesus, go all the way. Don't let yourself fall into the minimum-standard mentality of discipleship. Good works and good plans are not enough for you. Settle for nothing less than following God's perfect will.

Time 2
COUNT THE COST

It's one thing to take a bold stand for Jesus, to lift the standard of Christ in whatever situation you find yourself. But the power of your witness comes from a life that backs up your words. A lot of people are kept from coming out of their foxholes because of a sin, a habit or an idol in their lives that they keep holding on to. But there is nothing in your life, nothing in this world, worth losing the gift of salvation and your relationship with Jesus Christ. Knowing Christ lives in your heart and your sins have been forgiven and put behind you means more than the approval and applause of all the world.

Everyone has made mistakes. A lot people have dark closets in their lives filled with some pretty ugly things. God not only wants to forgive you, he wants to help you clean out those closets so that you can stand before him saved, delivered and free. If you want change in your life:

1. Give your life unreservedly to Jesus Christ and ask him to fill you with the Holy Spirit. You're going to see some things begin to happen inside and outside. People may scoff at first, but soon they'll see that something real is happening.

Saul of Tarsus was a persecutor of Christians before he literally saw the light on the Damascus road. In fact, he was such a violent opponent of Jesus and the disciples in the beginning that at first few people would believe he had become a follower. But soon people began to see that Saul was for real. With the power of the Holy Spirit helping you to change, people will see that you're for real, too.

I've heard it said that some people have just enough religion to make them miserable. Serving Christ halfheartedly is misery. When you put away compromise and make Christ the Lord of your life, that's when it gets full. That's when it gets exciting.

2. Walk in the light. Get involved in an accountability group where you are able to fellowship with other believers and help each other stick to Bible reading and prayer commitments. Recommended reading: Lorraine Peterson's *If the Devil Made You Do It, You Blew It* (Bethany House, 1989).

3. *Don't get stuck.* If you struggle with an area of your life, whether it involves drinking, sexual temptation or anything you can't seem to take control of, take the steps needed to put God back in charge. Talk to a Christian counselor or your pastor and let them give you a hand.

DON'T BE DECEIVED BY A WITCH'S INVITATION
(The Simple Truth Is in Jesus)

Saul said to his attendants, "Find me a woman who is a medium, so I may go and inquire of her."

"There is one in Endor," they said.

So Saul disguised himself, putting on other clothes, and at night he and two men went to the woman. "Consult a spirit for me," he said, "and bring up for me the one I name." (1 Sam. 28:7–8)

How is it that someone like Saul, the king of Israel who had had such experiences with God, who was trained by the prophet Samuel, who had removed all the mediums and spiritists from the land (1 Sam. 28:3)—how could it be that Saul would seek guidance from the witch of Endor?

It seems unthinkable. But Saul's actions follow a predictable pattern. Look at the situation Saul found himself in:

When Saul saw the Philistine army, he was afraid; terror filled his heart. He inquired of the Lord, but the Lord did not answer him by dreams or Urim or prophets. (1 Sam. 28:5-6)

The medium was astonished when she saw what appeared to be the spirit of the prophet Samuel. "Why have you disturbed me by bringing me up?" asked Samuel. Listen to Saul's response:

"I am in great distress," Saul said. "The Philistines are fighting against me, and God has turned away from me. He no longer answers me, either by prophets or by dreams. So I have called on you to tell me what to do." (1 Sam. 28:15)

In days of desperation and decline, when people feel as if God has departed, they will try any means possible to reach out for the spiritual world. Often their sense of guilt and sin have become so great they feel there is no way to get back to God or to communicate with him. They believe God has departed from them and wants nothing more to do with them.

The good news is that God has made a way, a bridge between sinful man and a holy God. But if the true gospel is not preached, people are left believing that the God of the Bible is too holy and too far away. The gulf is too wide.

So they seek spiritual guidance from someone other than the one true and holy God. Many conclude that turning to the occult will give them easy access to the spiritual world. In a way that's right. It's not hard to get in, but the door locks behind you.

126

Having given up on God they look for another "medium" into the spiritual world. Desperation, decline and separation from God almost always lead individuals and nations to the occult. In the last days of the Roman Empire, interest in the occult grew. The same thing happened during Hitler's last days of ruling Nazi Germany.

This also was the case with Saul. Saul had blown it badly, and he knew it. He felt God had departed, and his kingdom was in decline and on the way to judgment. The Witch of Endor was the only ready access to the spiritual world he could think of.

The "Jesus" of the New Age

The American people are not lacking for interest in spiritual things. In fact it's everywhere you look. Ouija boards, astrological charts, fortune-tellers, *Dungeons and Dragons* books and video games. Almost every cartoon series created in the last several years has occultic overtones, if not the bold-faced practice of spiritualism and witchcraft. Celebrities like Dionne Warwick, Eric Estrada and LaToya Jackson advertise on television a 900-number to contact your personal psychic.

What does the Bible have to say about this? Here are a few examples:

> **Let no one be found among you . . . who practices divination or sorcery, interprets omens, engages in witchcraft, or casts spells, or who is a medium or spiritist or who consults the dead. Anyone who does these things is detestable to the Lord, and because of**

**these detestable practices the Lord your God will
drive out those nations before you. (Deut. 18:10-12)**

The part about God driving out the nations refers to their
expulsion from the promised land, so they would not corrupt the
people of God. Listen to what God said:

**I will set my face against the person who turns to
mediums and spiritists to prostitute himself by
following them, and I will cut him off from his
people. (Lev. 20:6)**

Just because something is supernatural doesn't mean it's from
God. Just because it's real doesn't mean it's good. AIDS is real, but
like bootleg spiritualism, it will destroy you. Jesus said, **"I am the
way and the truth and the life. No one comes to the Father
except through me" (John 14:6)**. In other words, there are a lot of
spiritual things you can get into, but if a spiritual experience is not
through Jesus Christ, no matter how good it appears, you are
dancing with the devil.

Everywhere we turn today we see evidence of the New Age
movement. New Age books, New Age paintings, New Age
seminars. *Billboard* magazine now publishes a weekly chart of the
top-ten New Age songs. Today more people are finding the
entrance into the occult through the New Age movement than by
any other means.

What exactly is the New Age movement? Though it's a deadly
deception, it is not easily identified. There is no single prophet or

leader and no central headquarters. But there are hundreds of groups that identify themselves as New Agers. Probably the more dangerous deceptions are the New Age spin-offs that market themselves as motivation, self-help or assertiveness training groups.

There are a few central ideas that make up the fundamental beliefs of the New Age movement. New Agers believe that we are in a two-thousand-year period called the *Pisces Age,* of which Christianity is a part. The New Age movement gets its name from the belief that we are on the verge of entering into a *new age,* the Age of Aquarius. This belief system originates in astrology and the signs of the zodiac.

Remember the song by the Fifth Dimension?

When the moon is in the seventh house,
And Jupiter aligns with Mars,
Then peace will guide the planets,
And love will steer the stars;
This is the dawning of the Age of Aquarius,
The Age of Aquarius. Aquarius, Aquarius.
Harmony and understanding,
Sympathy and trust abounding.
No more falsehoods or derisions,
Golden living dreams of vision,
Mystic crystal revelation,
And the mind's true liberation.
Aquarius.

(from "Age of Aquarius," by James Rado, Gerome Ragni, Galt MacDermot and Nat Shapiro)

Everything that is a part of the *old age,* including Christianity is the old way of thinking. Have you seen the bumper sticker that says *Visualize World Peace?* In this new age there will be world peace and harmony, brotherly love will overcome all division, and there will be a *heaven-on-earth* utopian society.

Sounds great, doesn't it?—a lot like what the Bible calls the millennium. Some people will even try to tell you that the New Age is the completion of Christianity.

Not hardly. New Agers believe this age of harmony and understanding will come about only when we have a one-world government and a one-world religion. Any independent religions and nationalities that refuse to blend into the melting pot are obstacles to the new world order.

Without doubt, this is the spirit of antichrist. But the New Age movement does not denounce Christianity or Jesus Christ. It supposedly accepts all religions, even parts of Christianity. They even say it is okay to worship Jesus, but not the same Jesus of the Bible. They talk of salvation, but not biblical salvation. When they use the word *atonement,* they do not mean a blood sacrifice for the sins of humanity. They mean *at-one-ment,* becoming one with God through means other than Christ's sacrifice.

New Agers believe there is a separation between God and humanity. But the ideas of sin, separation, God and humans are all redefined. God is not a personal, holy, righteous and just God. Humans have no sin nature, but are inherently good. And the separation is not a moral separation.

For New Agers, God is a pantheistic life force, everywhere and in everything. So the only separation between us and God is an awareness separation. Through self-realization and meditation we can attain *at-one-ment* or union with God. A savior is simply a teacher or guru who can show you the way to an awareness of your union with the force.

If that reminds you of Star Wars' Obi-Wan Kenobi, Yoda and "May the force be with you," you're getting the point. That and other movies like it are a mixed brew of Eastern mysticism and New Age theology.

So you see, it's not so simple to distinguish the Spirit of Christ from the spirit of antichrist. That's why it is important that Christians today be grounded in the knowledge of the truth. It is not enough to get excited at a Christian meeting. You have to know who you are following.

Recognizing the Lord's Standard

One of the greatest challenges of today is how to recognize the Lord's standard when it is raised. Christ or Antichrist—two different masters, two opposite agendas—you'd think it would be easy to tell the difference. But that is not the case.

There are standards raised all over the battlefield, hundreds of them, and all the banners look very much like the Lord's banner. Many of them signify allegiance to God and Jesus. Are they all merely different versions of the same thing, or is this a trick of the enemy?

The great challenge of our day is to determine which is the true banner of the Lord. Jesus also identified that as one characteristic of the last days. He warned his disciples:

At that time if anyone says to you, "Look, here is the Christ!" or, "There he is!" do not believe it. For false Christs and false prophets will appear and perform great signs and miracles to deceive even the elect—if that were possible. (Matt. 24:23-24)

The tactic of the enemy in the last days is to raise so many counterfeit banners that it is hard to distinguish the authentic one. There will be gospels that look like the truth, organizations that look like the church and saviors who sound something like Jesus. In the last days there will be millions preaching a gospel, but a different gospel; millions attending church, but a harlot church; and millions worshipping Jesus, but a different Jesus.

But if you are intimately acquainted with the authentic, you are best prepared to distinguish the counterfeit. U.S. Treasury agents train to spot counterfeit currency by studying intricate details of genuine bills. Yet, so many Christians are biblically illiterate when it comes to distinguishing between authentic and counterfeit Christianity. Maybe they seldom come face to face with challenges to their faith. Maybe it's happening to them all the time, and they don't even recognize it.

Some people have been Christians all their lives and have no intention of changing religions. They feel no need to study the essentials of authentic Christianity. That may or may not work for them. If you get a great hiding place, maybe the conflict never will find you. But I know this: If you are considering coming out of the foxhole and taking a stand, you've got to know *where* to stand. If you're going to be one of those who lifts the standard, rallies the troops and leads the charge, you've got to know which is the real standard, and which is the real Jesus.

Satan hopes to get as many sincere people as possible to rally to counterfeit banners, but in the end they will find they have been deceived. On the last day, many will ask in astonishment, "Lord, Lord, did we not prophesy in your name, and in your name drive out demons and perform many miracles?" And then [he] will tell them plainly, **"I never knew you. Away from me, you evildoers!" (Matt. 7:22-23)**.

"Jesus," they will say, "we followed you." But because of slick-sounding words of a false prophet who came in the Lord's name, they mistakenly followed another Jesus.

The Standard and Measure of All Truth

You can spend a lifetime searching the depths of truth about God and the gospel of Jesus Christ. But the fundamental standard and measure of God's truth and Satan's lie is summed up in the question Jesus asked Peter: "Who do men say that I am?" Some will say Jesus is a prophet. Some say he's a great teacher, a martyr or a guru. But Peter got it right: **"You are the Christ, the Son of the living God" (Matt. 16:16)**.

Cults, heresies and false religions veil their true beliefs in hopes of drawing Christians into their web. But their illegitimacy is revealed by their understanding of Jesus Christ.

The person and work of Jesus Christ is the standard or measuring stick by which everything else is measured. As we've seen, if the measuring stick is inaccurate, then everything measured by it will be inaccurate too. Jesus said, **"If then the light within you is darkness, how great is that darkness!" (Matt. 6:23)**. In other words, if you miss it on this first point, everything else is going to be off-track and set on a course headed for darkness and bondage. That's why it is important that there be no doubt in our minds about who Jesus is, what he has done for us and what he will do in the future. That's why the standard we raise and the truth we share with others must be clear.

"Who Do Men Say that I Am?"

Jesus Christ was God himself. Not one of a thousand gods, not part of a fuzzy divine force, but the third person of the Trinity— God the Father, Son and Holy Ghost. False prophets and pagan recruiters quickly agree that Jesus was God. But they usually mean one of two things:

1) Jesus is a god, just as all the rest of us are gods. For them, God is the sum total of all things and each of us are a part of God. The illustration they frequently use is that God is the ocean, and we are all drops of water in the ocean of God. Yes, they will say that Jesus is God, but they mean something totally different than what the Bible says.

2) Jesus is God, but Buddha, Mohammed and Krishna are incarnations of God, too.

Make no mistake. Jesus is the only-begotten son of God. John 3:16 literally means: God gave his only *unique* son to die for us. There is no other like him.

Jesus was God incarnate. God came to us in the flesh as a man. John explained it best:

> **In the beginning was the Word, and the Word was with God, and the Word was God. He was with God in the beginning . . . The Word became flesh and made his dwelling among us. We have seen his glory, the glory of the One and Only, who came from the Father, full of grace and truth. (John 1:1-2, 14)**

That God came to live among us—as true God and true man at the same time—is a fundamental test of true Christianity. In the early years of the Church, they battled heresies introduced by those who tried to blend mysticism with Christianity. Some taught that Jesus was truly God, but that he only appeared to be in human flesh. They denied his humanity. Others affirmed his humanity, but rejected his deity. In writing to the Church about discerning the spirit of antichrist, the apostle John said this:

> **This is how you can recognize the Spirit of God: Every spirit that acknowledges that Jesus Christ has come in the flesh is from God, but every spirit that does not acknowledge Jesus is not from God. This is the spirit of the antichrist, which you have heard is coming and even now is already in the world. You, dear children, are from God and have overcome them, because the one who is in you is greater than the one who is in the world. (1 John 4:2-4)**

135

When John says *the one who is in the world,* he refers to the spirit of antichrist who is in the world.

Jesus died for our sin. The blood Christ shed on the cross was a guilt offering for the sins of every person. Forgiveness and righteousness are offered to every person who by faith in Christ's name receives these gifts. Be aware that those who agree that Jesus died for us might mean something totally different: Died only as a result of man's sin, or died as a martyred teacher, died as an example, a moral influence. That is quite different from dying as atoning sacrifice for our sin.

For New Agers and an assortment of eastern mystic cults, undoubtedly there is a gap between God and humanity. But the separation is caused by our lack of awareness, not our sin. Isaiah said:

Surely the arm of the Lord is not too short to save, nor his ear too dull to hear. But your iniquities have separated you from your God; your sins have hidden his face from you, so that he will not hear. (Isa. 59:1-2)

The good news is this: our separation and guilt are removed. Jesus, the perfect lamb without sin, gave himself as a sin offering for us.

Jesus Christ died and rose from the dead. He didn't faint, swoon or revive from a coma. *He was dead!* Jesus brought people back from the dead—like Lazarus, for example. But all of these people eventually died again. Jesus was resurrected with a glorified body, and he will live forever. That is the same thing that happens to all who accept Christ as their Savior. More than anything else, this bodily resurrection sets apart Jesus from all religious prophets, teachers, gurus and so-called ascended masters. And on the bodily resurrection of Jesus Christ the whole of Christianity rests. Don't be confused about this point.

Jesus is Lord. What do we mean when we say that? Philippians 2 says that as a reward for humbling himself and taking on the form of a human servant, God the Father exalted Jesus to be Lord of all that is in heaven and on earth.

> **[Jesus] made himself nothing, taking the very nature of a servant, being made in human likeness. And being found in appearance as a man, he humbled himself and became obedient to death—even death on a cross! Therefore God exalted him to the highest place and gave him the name that is above every name, that at the name of Jesus every knee should bow, in heaven and on earth and under the earth, and every tongue confess that Jesus Christ is Lord ... (Phil. 2:7-11)**

All judgment and authority have been given to the Son. When this world is over, it will not be the Father who will judge the world. He has assigned that privilege to the Son.

> **For he has set a day when he will judge the world with justice by the man he has appointed. He has**

given proof of this to all men by raising him from the dead. (Acts 17:31)

Jesus Christ will judge every angel and demon, as well as the deepest thought and intent of each person's heart. That is a scary thought for those who have rejected the blood of Christ shed for their sin. Scripture says every knee shall bow before Jesus, for he has been given all authority in heaven and on earth.

One Great Confession

Don't major on the minors in your dealings with other believers. We Christians cannot fight among ourselves without being overrun by the enemies of righteousness. A house divided against itself cannot stand, Scripture says. It doesn't matter as much whether we all believe the same about predestination and free will, the last days or church order. As believers we must realize that those of us who worship the Lamb on the throne are identified with and related to each other. We rally together under the banner of Jesus Christ—who is God come in the flesh, crucified for our sins, risen from the dead and coming again as Lord and Judge of the earth.

The power of the gospel is the person and work of Jesus Christ. That is our standard, and that is the banner we must lift up. We Christians must turn our focus to Jesus Christ himself and rally to that banner!

Time 2
MAKE IT HAPPEN

1. Are you slipping? Clear out New Age and occultic materials from your house, room and school locker. Ouija boards, tarot cards and jewelry with symbols you know are from the occult have no place in the life of a committed follower of Christ.

2. Be aware of those around you. Don't fill your life with people who are into the occult and other dark practices, even if they laugh and say they don't really believe in it. Don't get sucked in by lies that dabbling in seances or other occultic games and practices are harmless.

3. Forget Santa Claus and the Easter Bunny! Both are diversions from the truth and from the real reason for the seasons.

Easter is the time of the year when Christians celebrate the resurrection of Jesus Christ. *That* is cultural and historical fact. Every time Easter, or Christmas for that matter, rolls around, students and teachers have an opportunity to present the gospel of Jesus Christ. The resurrection of Easter and the virgin birth of Christmas are educational, historical facts, and well within the bounds of appropriate topics for discussion in public schools.

If you discuss the origin and history of these holidays, also include the reasons Christians believe in the virgin birth and the resurrection. If you have a Christian teacher or one who is open to discussion and debate, you will be allowed to present this in your classroom, or maybe to the entire student body!

Students in Christian schools also need to hear the evidence for the virgin birth and the resurrection. Even though the essential elements of the Christian faith are not attacked in Christian schools, that doesn't mean every person in those schools is a committed disciple of Jesus Christ. Just because a person attends a Christian school doesn't mean he or she has a firm, thought-out belief in Jesus Christ and what the Bible says about him.

You can get information on the history of Christmas and Easter from the encyclopedia. The best and easiest source for the reasons Christians believe in the virgin birth and the resurrection is Josh McDowell's *Evidence That Demands a Verdict.* This material is outlined, which makes it easy to adapt for debates, presentations and term papers.

Is This Kind of Discussion Legal?

You bet it is. On December 3, 1993, the American Center for Law and Justice (ACLJ) sent a three-page letter to each of the the 14,766 school superintendents in the United States. The letter outlines legal precedents for religious discussion in classrooms. Here are a couple of quotes from that letter:

> *The Supreme Court said, "It certainly may be said that the Bible is worthy of study for its literary and historic qualities. Nothing we have said here indicates that such a study of the Bible or of religion, when presented objectively as part of a secular program of*

education, may not be effected consistently with the First Amendment" (**School District of Abington Township v. Schempp**).

In **Stone v. Graham**, *the Supreme Court said, "The Bible may constitutionally be used in an appropriate study of history, civilization, ethics, comparative religion, or the like."*

For a copy of the entire letter, contact your school superintendent or

ACLJ
P.O. Box 64429
Virginia Beach, VA 23467
(phone) 804-523-7570

GO INTO ALL THE WORLD AND PREACH THE GOSPEL
(But Don't Give Up on Your Old Friends)

From the time I was eleven years old, my mother worked as a professional musician, always in all-girl bands. That made them unique, and it always opened doors for work. I had known Charlene, one of my mother's musician friends, since I was a kid. She was a dynamite guitar player, and when she sang, she sounded like Roberta Flack.

After I was saved, I quit singing in bars and started doing Christian music. I did not yet have an album and I ministered mostly in small churches. A couple of years after I became a Christian, I was invited to go to Hawaii to sing at a Christian conference.

It had been six years since I'd seen Charlene, and I heard she was performing in Hawaii. So while there, I wanted to find this woman who had taught me as a kid to play guitar, because I wanted to tell her about Jesus.

I called and asked her to attend my concert in this little church. She wouldn't come. I tried to get her to at least meet me at the hotel. She wouldn't do that either. Finally she said, "Why don't you come to see me? I'm working in a place called Lyn's Cocktail Lounge."

"Sure, I'd love to come," I told her. "I'll be there right after my concert."

There were about sixty to eighty people attending the Christian conference where I sang. After I finished, I told them that I felt the Lord leading me to go witness at a bar. I asked how many wanted to go with me. Everyone's hand went up.

"My friend is going to want me to sing," I said. "The place is called Lyn's Cocktail Lounge. If you want to go, meet me in the corner."

I could hear people starting to murmur. After the meeting I was told that Lyn's Cocktail Lounge was a gay bar and one of the seediest places in Waikiki.

Only three people went with me, and two of them told me they were only going along to drive. The only person who was going in with me was a little Hawaiian lady with tattoos all over her arms.

"I was a lesbian before I was saved," she said. "I used to hang out at that place, and I know all those people." So we all piled into a VW bug and headed for Lyn's.

When we walked into the place, everyone turned to look at us and check us out. I thought of all those old westerns I used to watch—*Comancheros*, *El Dorado*—and I did my best John Wayne imitation as I strolled in. I was trying to send a message to everyone: *Don't even think about it.* As soon as we got in, my lone companion deserted me. "I'm going to sit in the back," she said. "I'll cheer for you."

Charlene was shocked when I came in. She'd heard I had become a Christian, and never imagined I would actually come to a gay bar. She got up and sang her songs, and, as always, she was great. Then she asked *me* to come up and sing. I was nervous and reluctant, but finally I decided that she could use another surprise.

"Do you know how to play 'Danny Boy'?" I asked. As Charlene played the guitar, I started singing with all my heart the words that Dottie Rambo wrote to that old tune:

Amazing grace shall always be my song of praise.
For it was grace that bought my liberty.
I'll never know just why Christ came to love me so.
He looked beyond my faults and saw my need.

("He Looked Beyond My Faults,"
by Dottie Rambo)

When I got to "he looked beyond my faults and saw my need," I heard someone over in the corner shout, "Hallelujah!" That was a little unexpected. I knew it wasn't the woman who came with me.

I kept singing, "I shall forever lift my eyes to Calvary."

I heard the voice again, "Praise the Lord."

"I'll never know just how Christ came to love me so."

Again—"Hallelujah."

As I walked off the stage, the woman who was praising the

Lord came up, hugged me and introduced herself. She was an ex-roller-derby star who had gotten saved. She said that she came in there to pass out tracts, and was praying the Lord would send someone to encourage her.

"When you started singing," she said, "everyone got really quiet. I've never had more boldness than I had tonight."

Charlene was so touched by the song that she'd started to cry. We decided that we, along with her friend, would go someplace where we could talk.

"Do you mind if I bring some beer?" she asked.

"Okay. Whatever," I said, reluctantly.

So she brought a six-pack. Charlene only drank one beer, though she was used to downing a couple of six-packs a night. Then she pulled out her guitar, and we all started singing. My mother had sent her a tape of one of my Christian concerts, so she knew my songs. So there we all were, sitting around singing gospel songs. Both of them started crying again, and I led Charlene's friend to the Lord that night.

I've stayed in contact with Charlene through the years. It was about five years later when, over the telephone, I led her to the Lord. Charlene's name is now written in the Lamb's Book of Life!

It's easy to write off people. But almost everyone comes to Christ because of someone who brings them. It doesn't matter how far away they have gone or how many times they have rejected Christ. There's always hope. Don't give up on your old friends!

Are Your Friends Confused About You?

Being born-again, forgiven of your sins and in a personal relationship with Jesus Christ is the greatest thing that can happen to anyone. Most of the time people are so excited about this new life they have found, they can't wait to preach to their old friends. Unfortunately, some of these old friends are left a little puzzled about what's going on.

All they know is that their old buddy suddenly quit hanging around them. Nobody has seen him since the day he came back and started talking like a television preacher. He told them they were going to hell if they didn't get saved that minute. Everyone was pretty blown-away by the whole thing. For the most part they wrote him off and determined to stay away from his Bible study group. They didn't want to lose any more friends.

It takes boldness to go into a group of hardened sinners to preach the gospel. It also takes courage to be the friend of sinners. Jesus endured a lot of criticism for his relationships. They said of him:

> **For John came neither eating nor drinking, and they say, "He has a demon." The Son of Man came eating and drinking, and they say, "Here is a glutton and a drunkard, a friend of tax collectors and 'sinners.'"** (Matt. 11:18-19)

Jesus always hung out with sinners, prostitutes, cheaters and poor people. The religious people turned up their noses at that sort of thing. They thought righteousness meant having nothing to do with such riffraff. They completely separated themselves from those unsanctified people. In the end their exclusiveness caused them to be irrelevant to the common people. But Jesus spoke the language of average people and became their friend. What finally did him in was the Pharisees's jealousy of Jesus' ability to relate to sinners and common people.

Aren't you glad that God didn't give up on you after you turned down your first chance to accept Christ as your Savior? The love of God continues to pursue us, even after we reject him over and over. I know of people who prayed and witnessed to a friend for twenty years before they came to Christ. They just wouldn't let them go. I also know of situations where someone gave an old friend one ultimatum, and after that, never spoke to them again. That's very *religious*, but not very *Christ-like*.

Jesus came to *seek* and to save those who were lost. When they criticized him for attending a banquet of sinners and tax-gathers, Jesus said:

"It is not the healthy who need a doctor, but the sick. But go and learn what this means: 'I desire mercy, not sacrifice.'" (Matt. 9:12-13)

The Pharisees made all kinds of sacrifices to be holy. The problem was, though, they didn't love people. They held in contempt those who were not as holy or dedicated as they were. True spirituality is revealed not by how separate we can become from sinners, but by how effectively we can show the love of Christ to those who are far away from him.

Go into All the World

Most people who need to hear about Jesus Christ will never come to a church, or even to a Christian concert. Christians need to go where the people are.

I recently felt God leading me to go out into the streets where people actually live and congregate. Our first such venture was McComb's Dam Park across from Yankee Stadium in the Bronx. It was a Holy Ghost attack on "Fort Apache." We had twelve thousand come to hear the gospel in one of the highest crime areas of our nation.

When it came time for the altar call, the people literally pushed back the police barricades to get to the front. The three hundred police officers surrounding the park were amazed that an event like this could take place in such a high crime area. Some of the police officers themselves got saved.

In a place filled with crime, drugs and violence, you'd think people would not be interested in the gospel. *Wrong.* Those who live in darkness are often the most desperate for a glimmer of light and hope.

On March 10, 1993, we set up shop on Daytona Beach, Florida. *Beach Reach '93* turned out to be a tremendous success. Nearly 400,000 high school and college students crowded the beaches of Daytona to party, get drunk and score on drugs, sex and rock 'n roll. The stage was set for three weeks of well-planned carnality. What better place for the gospel of Jesus Christ to be presented? With MTV and the Playboy Channel set up within a hundred yards of us, we preached the gospel, led people to Christ, prayed for the sick and entertained the people—all at the same time. The Chamber of Commerce and the police department told us that we had a total of fifteen thousand listeners throughout the day. That doesn't count the many others who came within a mile of our speakers and inadvertently heard the good news!

The altar call that evening was a little unusual because we had no room for counseling. I led those who came in a sinner's prayer and invited them to stay for a special counseling session later. Three hundred people prayed with me and hung around for more counseling.

Don't let the devil convince you that people do not want to hear the gospel. Some Christians have so much faith in people's unwillingness to listen to the gospel, they never share the gospel with anyone. Whether it's in the Bronx, or during spring break at Daytona Beach, or at Lyn's Cocktail Lounge, there are people who want to hear the good news.

Persecution Complex

Jesus told a parable about a nobleman who went to a distant country to receive a kingdom for himself. The nobleman called ten of his servants and gave them each ten minas (one mina is equal to one-hundred-day's wages) with the instructions:

> **"Put this money to work," he said, "until I come back." But his subjects hated him and sent a delegation after him to say, "We don't want this man to be our king." (Luke 19:13–14)**

Most of the servants did pretty well. Some gained ten more minas, some gained five. But there was one servant who was too afraid to go out and do business with those people of the kingdom who hated their master. What he had was taken away from him.

A lot of people fail to do the Lord's business because they fear that everyone hates their master, and they assume that none of them want to hear what they have to say about God. Some people are persecuted for being Christians, but it's mainly in their own minds. They're sure that no one would like them if they knew they were Christians, and so they withdraw. They never get involved with what other people are doing, and they never get to know anyone who isn't in their church group. They isolate themselves from the world, not because they want to be holy, but because they are afraid.

Be bold about your faith and proud to be a disciple of Jesus. If you are convinced people won't accept you, they probably won't. If you are insecure and ashamed about being a Christian, what will non-believers think? Why should they want to be a Christian if those who are Christians are not excited about it?

Some believers make assumptions about those who would not be interested in hearing the gospel. But not the kids at Christian Chapel in Walnut Valley, California. Of the seven hundred teens who attend the weekly youth meeting, fifty percent are black and forty percent are Hispanic. Most once were involved in gangs. Many of them say they'd be dead by now if they hadn't found Jesus. One girl brought a hundred teenagers to the church. A varsity cheerleader at Nogales High School started a Bible club.

Skin-heads, neo-Nazis and gang members frequently attend the Bible studies, as well as the Christian Chapel meetings, and some have given their lives to Christ.[1]

Go In With the Flag Flying High!

Don't ever try to be a friend of sinners by compromising your commitment to Christ or by hiding your light under a basket. Put your light out where everyone can see it. Christians who are friends of sinners in the way Jesus Christ was always go in with the flag flying high. They are up-front about being followers of Jesus.

When Britt Woodall, a student at the University of Florida, gave his life to Christ, his first inclination was to move out of his fraternity house. But he began to pray about it. Sometimes people stay in their old environments because they have not made a complete commitment and are unwilling to submit areas of their lives to the Lordship of Jesus Christ. But Britt's commitment was without reservation, and as he prayed, he felt God wanted him to stay. In the year that followed, his fraternity brothers came to know Britt as a *Bible reading, midnight praying, devil-casting-out, morally pure, praying-for-the-sick, sincere, genuine Christian.* That year, dozens of young men in that frat house attended the Bible study in Britt's room, and several of them gave their lives to Jesus Christ. There was no question about where Britt stood. He maintained many friendships, but he did *not* hide his light. He flew the flag high.

The Public School Mission Field

Mark 16:15 says that we are to go into all the world and preach the gospel. Yet there are some places where that is almost impossible. Sadly, one of those strongholds is our high schools.

Eighty-five percent of people who make commitments to Christ do so by the age of eighteen. That's why it is important that Christian teenagers and adults work together to push down the doors that keep evangelism out of high schools.

When prayer was taken out of the classroom, that decision by the Supreme Court started a process of erosion. In 1963, the Supreme Court ruled that a prayer read over a public address system in an elementary school was unconstitutional on the grounds that it "violated the separation of church and state." Surprisingly, that phrase—*separation of church and state*—does not appear in the Constitution of the United States. It is found, however, in the constitution of the former Soviet Union. Our own First Amendment clearly states that "Congress shall make no law respecting the establishment of religion, or the free exercise thereof . . . "

In the next year, the high court ruled that Bible reading was unconstitutional. In 1987, the Supreme Court said you cannot teach the biblical account of creation without violating this supposed separation of church and state.

If you still think that none of this is a big deal, look what's happened during that time. According to a National Association of Educators' survey, the biggest problems in schools in the '40s and '50s were talking, chewing gum and running in the halls. When that survey was conducted in 1989, what were the schools' biggest problems? Drug abuse, suicide, rape and violence. A big, dark vacuum was created when prayer was removed, and it was filled with militant secularism and all its fruits.

You never know what will happen when one person steps out in faith. Not long ago, Bridget Mergens and seven of her friends decided to start a Christian club at their school in Omaha, Nebraska. They were denied permission. With the help of the Virginia-based National Legal Foundation, Bridget filed a religious discrimination suit against the local school board.[2]

In 1990, Jay Sekulow, chief legal counsel for Christian Advocates Serving Evangelism (CASE), went to the Supreme Court on behalf of the group of students in Omaha. Eight out of nine justices ruled in favor of the Christian high school students. The *Mergens v. Westside Board of Education* decision recognized the right of Christian student groups to have equal access to public school facilities.

With that decision, an entire mission field opened. Now the gospel can be freely proclaimed on the over twenty thousand public high schools.

We only need some radically saved teenagers who will put their heads and hearts together and organize themselves to take the gospel to their schools. In the sixteen months following that court decision, ten thousand Bible clubs were formed in public high schools. Almost all of them have had evangelism as their primary focus.

Since the *Mergens v. Westside* decision in 1991, CASE has received twenty-five to thirty calls for help each week. Every one of the cases has ended successfully, and most of them did not have to go to court. CASE has recently changed its name to The American Center for Law and Justice.[3]

There were only a few Christian students at Dallas High School in Dallas, Oregon, who wanted something good to happen in their school. They thought they were all alone. Nevertheless, three students started a Bible club. The first week, forty people showed up. The second week there were sixty. The third week, eighty, and on the fifth week there were 130 students at the Youth Alive Bible Club. That's one-fourth of the entire student body!

One student explained how the Youth Alive Bible Club got started:

> *It just goes to show what happens when you follow God's direction. It's not our doing. God talked to one girl, Cherese, and she talked to us. We followed his will, and everything fell into place. And look what God did in the assembly.*

Another student said, "When you see all these people out here, it's like peer pressure in reverse."

You don't have to be a five-star Christian evangelist to get something going. In December 1992, Ryan Galvan, a quiet fourteen-year-old, started The Lord's Campus Club during lunch hour at Hillside Junior High in Simi Valley, California. Ryan reported in the spring of 1993, "Fifty kids got saved in the last five months."[4]

In March of 1993, an estimated one million teens gathered at fifty thousand locations for a nationwide pizza party that was linked by a live satellite broadcast. Popular youth evangelist Josh McDowell preached, and surveys show that an average of three teens at each party made first-time commitments to Christ.[5]

The Mississippi Uprising

Toward the end of 1993, a group of students at Wingfield High School in Jackson, Mississippi, approached the principal, Dr. Bishop Knox, with a request. They wanted to say a prayer over the public address system at the beginning of the school day. This was *student*-initiated prayer, not *school*-initiated prayer. Dr. Knox knew that in 1992 a U.S. Circuit Court of Appeals in New Orleans ruled that prayer was permissible at graduation ceremonies if it was non-proselytizing, non-sectarian, and if students initiated and led it. Dr. Knox put it to a vote. The results were 490 in favor and 96 opposed. After explaining to the students the parameters they had to stay within, he gave them permission to go ahead. The school day began with the following prayer over the public address system:

> *Almighty God, we ask that you bless our parents, teachers and country throughout the day. In your name we pray. Amen.*

After three days, the ACLU got involved. The prayers were discontinued. Dr. Knox was suspended, and then fired. The students took a poll that overwhelmingly supported the principal.

The *Clarion-Ledger,* Jackson's leading newspaper, conducted a telephone survey. Over ninety-seven percent of the 2,500 people polled supported the principal felt he should not have been suspended.

The following week over four thousand people met on the steps of the state capitol in Jackson to protest. The students at Wingfield High participated in a mass walk-out to support the principal. State Senator Mike Gunn announced that he was introducing a bill that would withhold state funding from schools that denied students their constitutional rights to pray and have Bible clubs. [6]

Friends, the tide is turning. But it turns only when people take a stand. Multitudes are ready to come to Christ, but they only come when someone shares the gospel. I challenge you to become a bold witness, be a friend of sinners and fly the flag high!

Time 2
LET YOUR LIGHT
SHINE

The greatest experience you will ever have is leading someone to Christ and seeing their life transformed. There is nothing in the world like it.

1.   If there's not a Bible Club in your school, on your campus, at your office or in your neighborhood . . . START ONE! If there is one, get in it and bring all your friends. Bring those who most people have already given up on. Gang members, skin-heads, druggies, athletes, intellectuals and social elite all need the Lord. And they are all more interested than they let on.

2.   Take summer trips and vacations for Christ. One way you can stretch your spiritual wings is to commit your summer, your spring break or vacation to going on a mission trip. Often, your church or your denomination will organize trips. You can also work with other short-term mission organizations. Your life will certainly be changed. It's an experience that can break the yoke of fear and intimidation you may feel about sharing the gospel. Listed below are some non-denominational organizations that offer short-term mission programs:

Young Life
P.O. Box 520
Colorado Springs, CO 80901-0520

Youth for Christ International
6890 S. Tucson Way, Ste. 205
Englewood, CO 80112-3923

Youth With A Mission
P.O. Box 4600
Lindale, TX 75712-4600

Mercy Ships
P.O. Box 2020
Lindale, TX 75771

Campus Crusade for Christ
Summer Missions (foreign)
Dept. 2550
100 Sunport Lane
Orlando, FL 32809-7875

Last Days Ministries
P.O. Box 40
Lindale, TX 75771-0040

Celebrant Singers
P.O. Box 1416
Visalia, CA 93279

Habitat for Humanity
Habitat & Church Sts.
Americus, GA 31709-6935

Teen Mania Missions
P.O. Box 700721
Tulsa, OK 74170-0721

RAISE THE STANDARD OF RADICAL RIGHTEOUSNESS
(It's Okay to Say No)

When we begin to talk about God's moral standards, people immediately fast-forward to one conclusion, the wrong one—they think our purpose is to keep people from having any fun.

The picture most people have of Christians is of a group of people all dressed in their Sunday clothes dragging around with long faces and leading boring lives, while congratulating each other on how much better we are than other people. I guess there are some Christians who give that impression. But if Jesus did nothing else, he made it clear that those who are into rules and regulations without *religion of the heart* are missing the point.

Christianity is about forgiveness and abundant life. It's about loving God and loving others.

It's an abundant, exciting life, with love, joy, peace. It sounds great. But too many people think you can't have those things unless you set aside all this *biblical morality stuff*. They are confused, thinking that God is up in heaven trying to keep people from enjoying life.

In fact, the opposite is true. God made the rules because he loves us. Animals are directed by their instincts, but we are free moral agents. Freedom is that part of our humanity that makes us special. But we can also use that great gift to destroy ourselves. Electricity has tremendous benefits, but it also will fry you if you stick your finger in the socket.

Sex is the same way. We live in a generation that is trying to cast off all moral and sexual restraints, and as a result, people's lives, homes and families are being devastated.

Truth or Consequences?

God's moral law is absolute, immovable and eternal, and not just because he is bigger than we are. It's because he is better and smarter than we are. Sometimes, law is imposed by the guy who has the bigger club. But God has established his law forever because it's right, and it's for our good.

There are consequences of rejecting the truth about God and his moral standards. If you determine to ignore those laws, you'll only destroy yourself. Listen to the way one girl put it:

> *Hindsight's better than foresight. I used to wonder what that meant. Now I understand because it's so easy for me to look back and see where I went wrong.*
>
> *You know, first of all, my parents said wait until you're married. I was so confused. My teachers were*

telling me wait until you are mature. My friends were saying wait until tonight.

When I got pregnant, all of those same people were now saying the same thing—"You're too young to be a mother. You've got your whole life in front of you."

I listened to them then, and got an abortion. The second time, I thought that Tommy was going to marry me. But no, that was dumb. So the third time I did what I wanted. I kept the baby, and I'm glad that I did. He's the light of my life. I mean it's not easy being a mother. I still continue my education, and I hold down a job, but I'm mature now.

I'm fifteen. It's not like I don't know how to take care of myself.

The struggle you have with temptation is nothing like the struggle you will have with the consequences of giving in to those temptations. There are physical, emotional and spiritual results that will live with you, sometimes forever.

The physical effect of premarital or extra-marital sex are, among other things, an assortment of sexually transmitted diseases, only one of which is the deadly AIDS virus. Right now, *over one million* Americans are said to be HIV-positive, and *three thousand* new cases are reported each month. People who are HIV-positive, those infected with AIDS, show no symptoms in the first stages, yet they can pass the virus to others through sexual contact. One survey revealed that in the United States, sixty percent of high school girls and seventy percent of high school boys are sexually active. Forty percent of those active have had sex with four to six partners.

No one knows the extent to which AIDS has spread throughout our increasingly promiscuous society. A couple of years ago experts at the Centers for Disease Control estimated that the total number of HIV-infected persons was about 1.5 million. That's frightening. They arrived at that number by assuming that the number of people carrying the virus was fifty times the thirty thousand cases of full-blown AIDS. Today the number of people with full-blown AIDS is almost ten times greater, 250,000, but the estimated number of HIV carriers remains the same, 1.5 million.[1]

Besides the fatal AIDS virus, there are many other sexually transmitted diseases. What a shock it would be for a person to find out that from their first premarital sexual encounter they have walked away with a venereal disease that will be with them the rest of their life—and possibly even be passed on to their children! Yet that happens frequently.

Don't you think you'd better count the cost of sexual immorality?

Emotional Leftovers

People who engage in premarital or extra-marital sex are left with deep scars. There are a lot of things in life you can go back and do over. But you can never do something again for the first time. God's plan is for you to save that first time for marriage, for the person you are going to spend the rest of your life with.

Each time a person has premarital sex, it eats into their ability to be bonded together with their lifetime partner.

Do you not know that he who unites himself with a prostitute is one with her in body? . . . Flee from sexual immorality. All other sins a man commits are outside his body, but he who sins sexually sins against his own body. (1 Cor. 6:16, 18)

Attitudes about sex and the marriage covenant have now left us with over fifty percent of marriages in the first few years ending in divorce. With 1.1 million teenagers getting pregnant each year, it is evident that they have not learned the discipline needed for lifelong marriage. Rather, promiscuity is preparing them for divorce. People who are sexually active before marriage are sixty percent more likely to divorce than those who are virgins when they marry, according to a study by scholars at the National Center for Health Statistics and the University of Maryland.[2]

There is an emotional bond established when two people have sex. But having sex with many different people in your past weakens the bond sex was designed to put in your marriage.

Some people think that having sex will solidify their relationship. *If I have sex with him*, a girl might think, *he'll stick with me*. But the emotional bond established by sex outside of marriage is one of hurt, shame and the feeling of being used. He may hang around for the sex, but whatever relationship there is will deteriorate.

Sex is supposed to be the super-glue that holds a marriage together. But premarital sex undermines the trust required for any relationship to work.

For instance—suppose a guy says to his girlfriend or fiancee that he just can't wait until marriage. He can't help himself and wants to have sex. Later, they go ahead and get married. What has this guy demonstrated to his wife? It's that he cannot help himself. And if he can't restrain himself from violating someone he says he loves, when can he restrain himself? Premarital sex destroys the foundation of trust essential to make marriages work.

Forget Hollywood

Hell is where you will find yourself if you follow Hollywood's lead. People in the entertainment industry are quick to say that they are not shaping people's values and appetites, that they are only reflecting what's already out there in our society. If television has no power to change people's habits, why do corporations spend billions of dollars every year on television commercials? Because they know that television shapes the values and decisions of people.

Three areas are assaulted by contemporary movies and television programming. They are family, role models and the Christian lifestyle.

The Family: Two-thirds of all adults are married, and nearly all single people look forward to a healthy marriage relationship one day. However, whenever marriages are portrayed in popular movies they are represented as bad, psychotic or oppressive. The message is that there is only one context for true romance, and that is sex outside of marriage. Basically they say that marriage doesn't work. This doesn't reflect the values of two-thirds of all Americans, or the ideals of the remaining one-third.

Role Models: Hollywood role models, including Arnold Schwarzenegger, Sylvester Stallone, Chuck Norris, Jean-Claude Van Damme and Steven Seagal, have made their mark on American culture as cold, emotionless, killing machines who destroy human life with ruthless efficiency. Of course, they're pushed into violent behavior through adverse circumstances, but the result is always the same: death and destruction. I challenge you to go into a video arcade and count how many games are built around shooting, stabbing, punching and fighting. You may be surprised. Many pinball games now have a satanic twist to them. This is how we entertain ourselves.

Christian Lifestyle: Third, there's what can be called chronic Christian-bashing. Two recent Oscar-nominated performances were of people portraying Christian psychos—in *Misery* and a remake of the 1962 classic *Cape Fear*. To illustrate how things have changed let's take *Cape Fear* as an example. In the 1962 version, there were no family problems. However, the '92 version depicts a husband with adultery in his heart who emotionally batters his wife and daughter and has a very unhappy marriage. In 1962, the main character was a straight-up kind of guy. In 1992, he's unfaithful, dishonest and slimy. In 1962, Max Cady (the villain) was a bitter man bent on revenge. In 1992, he's a born-again Christian psychotic murderer who quotes Scriptures and speaks in tongues. As you see, movie and TV programming today displays a love affair with evil and a disdain for all that is good.

It's important to put the right things and the correct images in our minds. David said in Psalm 119:11: **"I have hidden your word in my heart that I might not sin against you."** God's Word steers us away from sin. Death, destruction and killing in the heart create crime. When the beautiful people in the movies glorify immorality, death and destruction, other people want to do it too.

Why is it that so many people act like animals when it comes to sex? They seem to have little conscience and even less ability to follow what conviction they do have. Jesus indicated that people are not defiled by what goes into their stomachs but by what comes out of their hearts. He said,

> **"What comes out of a man is what makes him 'unclean.' For from within, out of men's hearts, come evil thoughts, sexual immorality, theft, murder, adultery . . . All these evils come from inside and make a man 'unclean.' "** (Mark 7:20-23)

If you expose your mind and heart to a constant stream of sex, violence and cursing, you will eventually begin to act the same way. David wrote in the psalms,

> **I will walk in my house with blameless heart. I will set before my eyes no vile thing. (Ps. 101:2-3)**

The first step to moral purity in your body is to deal with your heart. And one of the first steps to doing that is to make a "covenant with your eyes" (Job 31:1). You have to determine that you will not expose your heart, mind and spirit to those things that are an abomination to the Lord.

The Dangers of Being Normal

The Bible says,

(Jesus Christ) gave himself for us to redeem us from all wickedness and to purify for himself a people that are his very own, eager to do what is good. (Titus 2:14)

If your goal is to be normal, then you're headed for big trouble. What is considered normal today actually is on the edge of immorality with an occasional venture into perversion.

The standards of virtue, faithfulness and saving yourself for your lifelong partner are considered by some to be completely out of reach and completely unrealistic. Consequently, they have given up on virtue and morality and are dealing with people on the lowest level—how to have safe sex.

Students are tired of being treated as if they are animals. If parents and educators don't have the guts to raise the standard, then some brave, intelligent students will have to.

One of them is a young woman I've heard about, Kristen Ericksen . . . But first, let me set the stage for you.

Into the Lion's Jaws

From the way some Christians in northern Virginia tell it, the whole situation felt like a set-up. The state of Virginia recently mandated that every school system had to adopt a sex-education curriculum, and this came about because certain liberal organizations had pushed a new law through the legislature. Christians in northern Virginia's Loudoun County became concerned when they learned that their own school board was flat-handedly rejecting a program that would teach students self-control and abstinence, in favor of a curriculum that taught no values and emphasized the use of condoms. Though the parents were supposed to have the right to review and approve the curriculum, something was going wrong.

The lesson plans they were allowed to see were unacceptable to most conservative parents, especially the Christians. But when some 350 parents and students appeared at an evening meeting at a local school to voice their opinions, they were shocked. They were told that this liberal curriculum was *already approved* by the school board. They could express their opinions if they wanted to, but the decision already had been made.

Imagine how you would feel if someone told you that you had no right to vote, and that your opinion basically was meaningless. The atmosphere in that school auditorium was charged with fire!

For several hours, parents and teachers stood before the school board and voiced their frustrations. But the board remained stoney-faced and adamant in their position: Students needed to know how to have "safe sex" by using condoms. The level of anger was rising.

In the middle of this charged atmosphere, a young woman, then a junior at Loudoun Valley High School, stood up. Kristen Ericksen is the daughter of an Assemblies of God pastor, and strong in her faith. I guess she had to be. Listen to what she said:

From the time I was little, my parents have always explained the facts of life to me one by one as I became old enough to understand them. They have helped me develop important morals and values. Kids today don't need a classroom lecture explaining how to use condoms. We already know about that stuff.

What we do need are role models with true morals and values. These role models include parents. In the long-run, we don't imitate some sex-education teacher. We imitate our role models, and we take on that role model's values.

Thank you for listening . . .

People who were there say there was a moment of stunned silence in the auditorium. What Kristen had said was the truth. Why were these liberal forces so eager to push their doctrine of "safe sex," when even students were saying, "Help us to say *no*. Help us to be strong."

If ever our country needed a sexual revolution, it is now. Others, like Kristen, need to stand up and say, "Yes, I have strong moral values, and I'm proud of it."

As Christian parents and students, *you* be the ones to change things. You be the ones to stand up and say, "We're going to set the standard."

Being normal means going along with the flow. But if you do that you are going to wind up in the same place with everyone else. It takes fewer people than you think to change what is considered cool from "anything goes sexuality" to virtue and virginity. But it never happens if people don't dig in their heels and refuse to be swept along with everyone else who has not enough backbone to say NO.

Self-respect is lost not only by giving yourself away physically. You can lose it by trying to be like everyone else and saying nothing.

What is worse than not being normal is having no personal identity—looking, walking, dressing and talking like everyone else, having no convictions of your own and only parroting what others say, being a clone, a mimic. You add nothing and you take nothing away. Such people are weak and without courage.

Simple Answers

We are a society at risk, assaulted from all directions by problems that seem unsolvable. But on every front, our problems are basically religious problems. Drugs, crime, divorce, AIDS, violence, the lack of productivity, educational ineffectiveness and a host of other difficulties that come from the breakdown of the family all are the results of the deterioration of character and morality.

Most everyone will agree with that. Consequently, public

school educators make feeble attempts to teach moral values to students without any mention or recognition of God. That's not only hard, that's logically impossible. Without God, morality and human values are only a myth.

Some people will argue that you don't have to have God to be moral. They are dead wrong! What morality exists in our society is there for two reasons:

1. There is still a lot of Christian influence around today.

2. Throughout our history Christianity has been so thoroughly engrained in American life, the memory of that heritage still imposes a moral influence.

In the preface to Herbert Schlossberg's *Idols for Destruction,* Judge Robert Bork wrote this:

> *Some few years ago friends whose judgment I greatly respect argued that religion constitutes the only reliable basis for morality and that when religion loses its hold on a society, standards of morality will gradually crumble. I objected that there were many moral people who are not at all religious; my friends replied that such people are living on the* **moral capital** *left by generations that believed there is a God and that he makes demands on us. The prospect, they said, was that the remaining moral capital would dwindle and our society become less moral. The course of society and culture has been as they predicted . . .* [3]

When I sing or I say, "We need God in America again," some people might smugly respond, "That's too simplistic! How unsophisticated can you be?"

Many so-called experts discuss complicated socio-economic theories and suggest even more complicated and expensive government programs to help people who, they say, are victims of one thing or another. They certainly wouldn't want to say that someone was wrong or bad, let alone sinful. Neither would they want to be so insensitive as to suggest that wicked people are responsible for their own actions. But all the secular social engineering over the last thirty years hasn't worked. If anything, it has made matters worse.

Sure, we have complex problems today. But multiple effects are the results of causes that are often very simple. One atom of enriched plutonium splits, releasing particles that collide with many other plutonium atoms causing them to split, releasing particles that collide with many other plutonium atoms, and so on. That is called a chain reaction and is the principle behind nuclear fission—atomic bombs.

What could have caused the massive and terrible destruction at Hiroshima? Simple—a plutonium atom split. Of course, that single initial act was tiny, but the process of fission that was set in motion was extremely complex and destructive. The further back you trace to the root cause of a chain reaction, the simpler the causes become.

Q: What has caused the problems in our culture?
A: We've turned away from God.

That is the simple answer, simple not because it is naive, but because it is fundamental.

Q: What do we need to do?
A: Put God in our world again.

Some people say the problems of teenage sexuality are complex. They're right—well, almost. The problems *caused by* premarital or extra-marital sexual activity are numerous and enormously complicated. But the answer is simple—not easy, but simple: Wait until marriage.

Q: How do we protect ourselves from the AIDS virus?
A: Abstinence before marriage and fidelity after marriage.

The ideas of those who reject God's laws have become so obviously ridiculous and the results of their philosophies so devastating, that people are beginning to realize that God's way was right all along. There is a growing movement among young people to commit themselves to wait for sex until marriage.

A. C. Green, who plays forward and center for the Phoenix Suns, has boldly proclaimed the gospel ever since he became a Christian at Oregon State University. A. C., a bachelor, has appeared on talk shows with Montel Williams, Chevy Chase,

James Dobson and others, talking about abstinence and the value of keeping yourself pure until you are married.

True Love Waits is a national campaign sponsored by The Baptist Sunday School Board. The year-long campaign is designed to challenge teenagers and college students to remain sexually pure until marriage. As part of the campaign, 500,000 teenagers from across the country are expected to sign covenant cards that state:

> *Believing that true love waits, I make a commitment to God, myself, those I date, my future mate, and my future children to be sexually pure until the day I enter a covenant marriage relationship.*[4]

As a part of the July 29, 1994 celebration ending the year-long campaign, several hundred thousand signed covenant cards collected from teenagers across the country will be displayed on the mall between the Washington Monument and the U.S. Capitol. Thousands of youths will gather around the cards for a time of prayer, followed by a concert featuring Steven Curtis Chapman, Petra and DeGarmo and Key.

Spiritual Consequences

The spiritual impact of premarital sex is that it shuts down our ability to communicate with God. It is like we are talking into a telephone when someone has cut the cord. Once you get cut off from God, then it is easy to go downhill fast.

In the midst of your temptations a voice will tell you over and over to go on—that it will be alright. But after the act, the deception will be removed, and you will feel the full weight of the guilt. Satan is not there to comfort you. He's just laughing. The goal of Satan is to kill, steal and destroy. Most of the time he does that by assisting you in destroying yourself.

King David was a man after God's own heart. Yet, he fell into adultery, and got another man's wife pregnant. Maybe a better way of putting it is that he jumped into adultery. To say that someone falls into adultery implies that it was an accident that was perhaps unavoidable. No, David plotted his scheme and eventually murdered the woman's husband to cover his sin.

David was like a lot of people who have thought that they were powerful enough or smart enough to get away with it. But God is no respecter of persons, and you cannot hide from him.

Like every other person, David suffered as a consequence of his sin. But eventually he came back to God through confession and deep repentance. He wrote a prayer in the form of a psalm:

Have mercy on me, O God, according to your unfailing love; according to your great compassion blot out my transgressions.

Wash away all my iniquity and cleanse me from my sin.

For I know my transgressions, and my sin is always before me.

Against you, you only, have I sinned and done what is evil in your sight, so that you are proved right when you speak and justified when you judge . . .

Hide your face from my sins and blot out all my iniquity.

Create in me a pure heart, O God, and renew a steadfast spirit within me . . .

Restore to me the joy of your salvation and grant me a willing spirit, to sustain me.

Then I will teach transgressors your ways, and sinners will turn back to you.

The sacrifices of God are a broken spirit; a broken and contrite heart, O God, you will not despise. (Ps. 51:1-4, 9-13, 17)

The Pharisees, who loved the rules more than they loved God, brought a woman before Jesus who had been caught in adultery. They wanted to stone her. But Jesus saw her heart and said, **"Neither do I condemn you. Go now and leave your life of sin"** (**John 8:11**). God desires to forgive us and restore us to wholeness.

The good news of the gospel is this: Jesus did not come to condemn the world but to save it. Jesus died on the cross so that your sins could be wiped away.

In Shakespeare's *MacBeth,* Lady MacBeth's overwhelming sense of guilt caused her to lose her mind. She imagined there was a spot on her hand and constantly rubbed it. But the spot could not be removed.[5]

Like the old hymn says:

What can wash away my sin? Nothing but the blood of Jesus.

> (from "Nothing but the Blood of Jesus,"
> by Robert Lowry)

No matter how hard you try to erase the guilt and condemnation of past sin, nothing wipes it out but the blood of Christ.

Without the cleansing blood of Jesus Christ, your sin and guilt will live with you for eternity. But when God forgives, it is complete. David again wrote in the psalms:

For as high as the heavens are above the earth, so great is his love for those who fear him; as far as the east is from the west, so far has he removed our transgressions from us. (Ps. 103:11-12)

Perhaps you, like David, have fallen, or rather, jumped into sin. God wants to cleanse you and give you a new start. Sometimes it is hard to come to God asking for forgiveness because you have such a hard time forgiving yourself or because you feel unworthy. You're right—you are unworthy. But your worth is now calculated by how much you are worth to God—enough to send his Son for you.

He also bore our iniquity:

We all, like sheep, have gone astray, each of us has turned to his own way; and the Lord has laid on him the iniquity of us all. (Isa. 53:6)

Jesus hung on the cross, humiliated before the world. People who have had illicit sex most of the time feel shame, as if they have been exposed to the world. Jesus not only bore our sin on the cross, but he also bore our shame.

Forgiveness comes by confessing your sin, repenting and asking God to cleanse you. First John 1:9 says, **"If we confess our sins, he is faithful and just and will forgive us our sins and purify us from all unrighteousness."** If you do this with a sincere heart, God will do for you what he did for David—he'll create in you a clean heart.

Time 2
FACE THE
FACTS OF LIFE

1. Churches, Christian parents and students cannot run from or ignore sexuality. Josh McDowell has two video series: *No! The Positive Answer* is aimed at teens themselves. *How to Help Your Child Say No to Sexual Pressure* is for parents and teens and has been seen in 30,000 churches. Contact Josh McDowell Ministries, P.O. Box 1000, Dallas, TX 75221-1000 or call the toll-free order processing line, 1-800-222-5674.

2. We also have two *Time 2* videos on teenage sexuality, entitled *Truth or Consequences, Part I & II.* All of these videos are great stuff for church youth groups or school Bible clubs. Contact us at Carman Ministries, P.O. Box 701050, Tulsa, OK 74170-1050 or call 1-800-79TIME2.

3. A. C. Green of the Phoenix Suns has produced a twenty-five minute video on abstinence, entitled *It Ain't Worth It.* The video ends with a rap performed by pro athletes Darrell Green (Washington Redskins), David Robinson (San Antonio Spurs), Barry Sanders (Detroit Lions) and

A. C. Contact A. C. Green Programs for Youth, 1-800-AC YOUTH.

4. We are going to have sex education in public schools. So Christian parents and students must to do everything we can to get the best material possible presented there.

Sex Respect, a three-part video series on abstinence-based sex education, is designed for use in public schools. It includes a student workbook and a teacher manual. Also check out this video for church groups, entitled *Chastity Challenge.* To order or for more information write *Sex Respect*, P.O. Box 349, Bradley, IL 60915-0349 or call 815/932-8389.

Postponing Sexual Involvement is an abstinence program used with impressive results in the Atlanta public school system. Write to Grady Health System, Teen Services Program, P.O. Box 26158, 80 Butler Street SE, Atlanta, GA 30335 or call 404/616-3513.

The *True Love Waits* campaign encouraged

young people to make a personal commitment that every unmarried Christian should make. You and your friends can make up your own card to sign:

> *Believing that true love waits, I make a commitment to God, myself, those I date, my future mate, and my future children to be sexually pure until the day I enter a covenant marriage relationship.*

For general information about the *True Love Waits* campaign, call Nancy Boehmer at 1-800-LUV-WAIT. To order campaign kits, call 1-800-458-2772.

10

WE'RE LIVING IN THE LAST DAYS
(But It's Not Over till It's Over)

How many "last days" are there anyway?

On the day of Pentecost, Peter stood, cited a prophecy from Joel and proclaimed that *they* were living in the last days. That was almost two thousand years ago! Either there were a lot of last days left, or each of those last days is pretty long. In either case, the last days began when Jesus rose from the dead and the Holy Spirit was poured out on the Church.

God doesn't judge time the way we do. God is eternal. He is not very very old, with no end to how old he will get. God is timeless, that is, he exists before, after and beyond time.

In our world of time and history, we see a long, complex series of events that follow one after another. God sees the whole parade of history from the beginning to the end, as if it were all happening now, right before his eyes.

Peter wrote this to some Christians who were anxious about how long it was taking for these last days to get over:

First of all, you must understand that in the last days scoffers will come . . . They will say, "Where is this 'coming' he promised? Ever since our fathers died, everything goes on as it has since the beginning of creation" . . . But do not forget this one thing, dear friends: With the Lord a day is like a thousand years, and a thousand years are like a day. (2 Pet. 3:3-4, 8)

Remember that God doesn't work on our timetable. We're like children watching a parade through a knothole in the fence. We can see only one part of the parade at a time, the part that's happening right in front of us. But if we climb a tall tree, we can see over the fence and all the way to the last float.

Has the end of the parade arrived at our doorstep? The Bible tells us the signs of the end times, and some clearly are taking place in the world today. But then only God really knows when the end will come.

All Dressed Up but Going Nowhere

Jesus said to his disciples:

"Therefore keep watch, because you do not know on what day your Lord will come." (Matt. 24:42)

It's ironic, but many times those who think they know when the Lord is coming have been so *alerted* that they forget what they are supposed to be doing when he comes.

As the last day approached, two hundred and fifty disciples put on white robes and ascended to the top of the hill to wait for the imminent return of Christ. It was October 22, 1844. A famous revivalist, William Miller, had studied the book of Daniel, made detailed calculations and discovered the day he thought Christ would return. For three years, he published material and lectured on his theory. Hundreds of thousands began to prepare for the end.[1]

They were alert, they were ready—and they were *wrong*.

This has happened over and over throughout history. According to Revelation 13:18, the man of sin, the Antichrist, will appear first. Some of those believed to be the Antichrist are Benito Mussolini, Adolf Hitler, Franklin D. Roosevelt, Henry Kissinger, John F. Kennedy, Anwar Sadat, Ronald Reagan and Mikhail Gorbachev. And with that belief came a prediction of the end of the world.

From the second century onward, there has been a continuous stream of end-time predictions that cite the sorry condition of the world, along with historical and natural events, as sure signs that they were living at the end of history. Some of those events thought to be the sure sign of the end were: the sacking of Rome by the Vandals in 410 A.D., the Inquisition in the thirteenth century, the French Revolution, the bubonic plague that killed a third of the world's population in the fourteenth century, the Hundred-Years War, the two World Wars of this century and, most recently, Desert Storm.

A few years ago, Edgar C. Wisenant, a retired NASA engineer, published and sold hundreds of thousands of copies of *88 Reasons Why the Rapture Will Be in 1988*. Wisenant spent fourteen years studying 886 biblical prophecies and finally arrived at September 11-13, 1988 as the time the church would be taken out of the world.[2] People who believed Wisenant made preparations for their departure, only to find that the Lord didn't come and that they were now going to have to pay for all the stuff they put on their credit cards.

Most recently a large group of Christians in Korea figured out when the Lord was returning, sold all their possessions and met together to wait for the rapture. Again they were disappointed.

So far, all who thought they knew have been wrong. History confirms what Jesus said: **"No one knows about that day or hour, not even the angels in heaven, nor the Son, but only the Father" (Matt. 24:36).**

What in the World Is Going On?

Some are convinced that the end of the world is near because things look really bad. This often has happened in the face of war or moral decline. Certainly the end of all things is at hand, they think. On the other hand, when God is moving everywhere in great power, they conclude that it certainly *must be* the last great end-time revival.

Don't get discouraged by the bad news of what is going on in your neighborhood or your nation. God is moving all over the world like never before.

It took us over a year of planning and negotiating to reserve the largest arena in South Africa, the Wanderers Cricket Stadium. It had never before been used for a concert. The official seating capacity was 46,814! It was a complex and complicated procedure, but the Lord was with us, and after a ton of red tape, the stage was set.

The day of the concert was unbelievable. People came from everywhere. Traffic in the surrounding areas and on the highway into the city came to a halt at 10 a.m. With traffic still backed up for blocks half an hour past the announced start time, the gates were simply thrown open for whoever could make it in. Over fifty thousand people came inside and thousands had to be turned away. It was the largest gathering for a solo musical event ever in South Africa. In the huge crowd that filled the stands and the cricket field was Nelson Mandela, as well as numerous representatives from government and political parties.

There is a tremendous hunger for God in South Africa, as there is in many nations in every part of the world. In 1982, for the first time in over a thousand years, the majority of Christians were not in the New World (North America and Europe) but in the Third World. The church of Jesus Christ quickly is becoming African, Latin American and Asian. The unstoppable gospel is spreading like wildfire all over the world.

Christianity v. Culture—Keeping Score

There is a cultural war going on in America today. Many groups are struggling to capture the high ground and raise their standard over the nation. But that does not necessarily mean that the number of committed Christians is declining. In the '50s and '60s Christianity was much more dominant in society. When a society is so influenced by cultural Christianity, it's hard to tell who is a sold-out disciple and who is going along with the crowd.

Today, there definitely are fewer nominal Christians sitting on the fence, not being committed either way. But the number of dedicated disciples is probably greater than ever.

An article in the April 5, 1993 edition of *Time* showed that traditional mainline denominations that have taken a liberal turn over the last decade have declined in membership by the millions. Six such denominations reported a combined net membership loss of 6.2 million since the mid-1960s. That represents a loss of over twenty percent.

At the same time, churches that were evangelical and theologically conservative (committed to biblical doctrines) showed tremendous growth.[3]

For the most part, churches on the decline are the ones that have compromised the gospel, rejected biblical morality and many of the fundamentals of the faith while embracing the social agenda of militant feminists and homosexuals. But the churches that preach the Word of God and win people to Jesus Christ are exploding.

Who Said Abandon Ship?

If that is the case, then why do we have such problems today? How is it that our culture has become so pagan and anti-Christian? The answer is simple. For the last twenty to thirty years, Christians in their excitement about the coming of the Lord have given up proclaiming their victory in all areas of life. They have abandoned the institutions and given them up to anti-Christian influences. That's why the entertainment industry, news media and educational system are polluted with such anti-Christian influences.

An example of how the enemy has come into the vacuum left by the retreating church is the motion picture industry. "Only a generation ago the church was effectively exerting its influence to redeem the values presented in the film industry," says Ted Baehr, founder and chairman of the Christian Film and Television Commission (CFTVC). Representatives from Protestant and Catholic churches evaluated movie scripts according to the Motion Picture Code, a standard that was in effect from 1930 to 1968. This helped the Motion Picture Association of America maintain the moral integrity of the productions of most of the major studios.

According to Baehr, a few months after the Protestant Film Office shut in 1966, the Church of Satan Film Office opened. Before long, homosexual activists, Marxists and other groups opened film offices to lobby for their points of view. Within two years of the church's withdrawal from Hollywood, movies glorified Satanism *(Rosemary's Baby),* homosexuality *(Midnight Cowboy)* and excessive violence *(The Wild Bunch).* Today more than sixty percent of movies are R-rated, most of them packed with sex and gore.[4]

Positions of power and influence were abandoned by Christians. Others have taken over by default. *And that is the reason for cultural decline.*

Many have the idea that if the Lord is coming soon and the

devil is destined to take over everything, then why polish brass on a sinking ship? Some people figure that the sooner the devil takes over everything, the sooner the Lord will return. I've even heard people criticize the efforts of Christians as if they were working against God's plans. *That* is stupid and presumptuous thinking, and by it many excuse themselves from the responsibilities God has given them.

In a sense the church is waiting on the hilltop, dressed in their white robes, while the devil is robbing their homes of everything they have. When the Lord didn't come, they went home to find it all gone—the schools, the culture, the nation. All those things that were given for the glory of Christ have been stolen and turned into weapons against Christians.

The Christians abandoned the ship!

Coming Out of Hiding

The apostle Paul said:

But thanks be to God, who always leads us in triumphal procession in Christ and through us spreads everywhere the fragrance of the knowledge of him. (2 Cor. 2:14)

Our goal is that the knowledge of God would be in every place. That doesn't just mean in every pew of your church. That means Christians should dedicate themselves to the cause of Christ as journalists, judges, teachers, leaders of business and industry. We need to take a stand and not be so timid. We cannot give up our nation without a fight.

When you are hiding in a foxhole, you don't know much about anyone else, only about those who are in your hole. There could be an army of tens of thousands hiding in holes, caves and trees, everyone thinking they are the only ones left.

That was the way it was with Elijah who faced the prophets of Baal, the anti-Christian king and the whole kingdom filled with idolatry and occultism. He faced them alone trusting only in the power of God.

You probably know this story. Elijah challenged the 450 prophets of Baal and the 400 prophets of Asherah who ate at the table of Jezebel. They built two altars, put a slaughtered ox on each one and took turns praying to their god. The prophets of Baal prayed, cried and cut themselves until noon. Then Elijah called on the Lord and the altar was consumed with fire.

Even after such a display of the power of God, Elijah was depressed and discouraged because he thought he alone was standing for the Lord. He had said to the people, **"I am the only one of the Lord's prophets left" (1 Kings 18:22)**. Later the Lord said to the discouraged Elijah, **"I reserve seven thousand in Israel—all whose knees have not bowed down to Baal and all whose mouths have not kissed him" (1 Kings 19:18)**.

I'm not suggesting you set up an altar in the reception area of your office building or in the principal's office. But you do need to take a stand and follow the captain of the Lord of Hosts, Jesus. The point of the story is that Elijah thought he was alone, the only one left. Yet, there were thousands who were laying low, just waiting for someone like Elijah to take a stand for righteousness.

It's always like that. It doesn't take a lot of people in any one place to raise the standard. People who will pick up the flag and lead the charge, not knowing if anyone is following, are a little bit crazy. At least that's the way the world and even some Christians look at them—as if they were Popeye, shouting crazily, "That's all I can stands, and I can't stands no more!"

God knows they love him, and they have to take a stand even if no one else does. They are people called and empowered by the Holy Spirit.

It doesn't take many people like that to take those kind of stands. But it takes millions of Christians who will dedicate themselves to a lifetime of service spreading the gospel in everything they do. We don't need *short-timers* but *lifers*, who have committed that everything they do will be for the kingdom. Perhaps they will study for ten years to be a doctor who advances the kingdom of God, or a judge, or a journalist or a missionary.

Whatever they do, their jobs are not for themselves. They are lifetime revolutionaries. We need a few to raise the flag, but we need millions of those kind of disciples.

Why Think About the Future?

Why should you want to buy a house if Jesus is coming back in a few short years or maybe a few months? Why go to college? Why prepare? Why have a savings account? Why prepare for the future or for your retirement?

It is not as important that we *know when he is coming* as it is that we *live our lives in the light of his coming*. But that doesn't mean we put on robes and go up the hill.

Jesus instructed us how we should prepare for his coming:

"Who then is the faithful and wise manager, whom the master puts in charge of his servants to give them their food allowance at the proper time? It will be good for that servant whom the master finds doing so when he returns." (Luke 12:42-43)

Here's what the Lord is looking for from us. Here is the kind of people we should be. When the Lord returns, we are to be doing whatever God's will is for us. If you are in school and you are preparing for a future, don't leave school. Prepare, because when he comes back, he is going to look and see who is faithful. Have you been a steward of what God has entrusted to you?

The expectation of the master's return caused them to get busy. The master was coming to call the stewards to account for what they had done with the opportunities entrusted to them. Many Christians today think of the return of the Lord only in terms of escape, and the more they think about it, the more unfaithful they become.

The Philistines assembled to fight Israel, with three thousand chariots, six thousand charioteers, and soldiers as numerous as the sand on the seashore . . . When the men of Israel saw that their situation was critical . . . they hid in caves and thickets, among the rocks, and in pits and cisterns. (1 Sam. 13:5-6)

Jonathan suggested to his armor-bearer that the *two of them* go over and attack the Philistines. **"Perhaps the Lord will act in our behalf. Nothing can hinder the Lord from saving, whether by many or by few," Jonathan said (1 Sam. 14:6).**

When they were spotted, the Philistines said, **"Look . . . the Hebrews are crawling out of the holes they were hiding in" (1 Sam. 14:11).** Jonathan and his armor-bearer went up and began to fight a garrison of about twenty men.

> **Then Saul and all his men assembled and went to the battle . . . Those Hebrews who had previously been with the Philistines . . . went over to the Israelites . . . When all the Israelites who had hidden in the hill country of Ephraim heard that the Philistines were on the run, they joined the battle in hot pursuit. So the Lord rescued Israel that day . . . (1 Sam. 14:20-23)**

Jonathan and his armor-bearer took a chance and made a stand. As a result thousands came out of hiding. Sometimes that's all it takes.

Who knows what the Lord will do if students begin to pray for their classmates and share the gospel with them? Who knows what will happen when people begin to do the same thing in their neighborhoods or at their jobs? Who knows what God might do through individuals who take a stand for righteousness in the community or roll up their sleeves to reach out to those who are in great need? What might God do through those who dedicate their lives, talents and careers to advancing the kingdom of God?

God is looking for someone to raise the standard where you live. Could he be looking for you?

Time 2
MAKE IT HAPPEN

I decide this day that with God's help:

•I will be bold and up-front about being a disciple of Jesus Christ, and I will bear his name proudly.

•I will no longer shrink back in the face of intimidation.

•I commit myself to a life of holiness and righteousness.

•I will seek, not God's permissive will, but his high calling.

•I commit the rest of my life to serving the Lord with my career, my talent and my life in whatever way he directs me.

•I determine to raise the standard of Christianity and to bear the colors, even if I have to do it alone.

Date _____

Signed _____

NOTES

Chapter 1

1. William J. Bennett, *The Book of Virtues* (Simon & Schuster, 1993).
2. *Christianity Today* (June 21, 1993) p. 46.
3. George Grant and Mark A. Horne, *Legislating Immorality* (Moody Press/Legacy Communications, 1993) p. 80.

Chapter 2

1. John W. Whitehead, *The Separation Illusion* (Mott Media, 1977) p. 18.
2. Michael Farris, *Where Do I Draw the Line* (Bethany House, 1992) p. 54.
3. "Christians in Court," *Charisma & Christian Life* (Dec. 1990) p. 66.
4. "Students Gain Rights," *Charisma & Christian Life* (Nov. 1990) p. 40.
5. Farris, *Where Do I Draw the Line,* p. 100.
6. Ibid, p. 104.
7. Jonathan Edwards, "Men, Naturally God's Enemies," *The Works of Jonathan Edwards, Vol. 2* (Banner of Truth, 1979) p. 132.
8. Ibid, p. 132
9. Brannon Howse, ed., *Cradle to College* (New Leaf Press,1993) pp. 43-45 and David Gyertson, ed., *Salt and Light* (Word, 1993) pp. 202-204.
10. "South Asia: Into the Heart of Darkness," *Charisma & Christian Life* (Jan. 1993) pp. 27-33.

Chapter 3

1. *People* (Oct. 4, 1993) p. 8.
2. *Time* (Dec. 9, 1991) p. 61.
3. Ibid.
4. David Barton, *America: To Pray or Not to Pray* (WallBuilder Press, 1991) p. 28.
5. James D. Richardson, *A Compilation of the Messages and Papers of the Presidents, 1789-1897* (Published by Authority of Congress, 1899), Vol. 1, p. 220.
6. Mark Rutland, *When the Devil Goes Too Far* (audio tape). Contact: The Trinity Foundation, Inc., 2290 South Volusia, Suite A, Orange City, FL 32763.
7. *Christian History*, Vol. VIII, no. 3, p. 27.
8. Harold A. Fischer, *Reviving Revivals,* p. 162.
9. *Christian History,* Vol. VIII, no. 3, p. 27.
10. W. A. Pratney, *Revival* (Whitaker House, 1983) p. 111.
11. *Christian History,* Vol. VIII, no. 3, p. 22.
12. Ibid, p. 25.
13. Ibid.
14. Ibid, p. 27.

Chapter 4

1. *A Revival Account—1970* (video) (Reel to Real Ministries, Cantoment, FL, 1988). For information on how to obtain a copy of this video, contact American Portrait Films, 503 East 20th Street, Cleveland, OH 44119.
2. Ibid.
3. Ibid.
4. J. Edwin Orr, *The Fervent Prayer* (Moody Press, 1974) p. 1.
5. *Christian History,* Vol. VIII, no. 3, p. 32.
6. *Eusebius's Ecclesiastical History* (Baker, 1981) pp. 75-79.
7. *The Christian in the Public School* (Student Action for Christ, Inc., Herrin, IL, 1983) p. 52.
8. David Barton, *To Pray or Not to Pray* (WallBuilder Press, 1991).

Chapter 5

1. Peter Kreeft, *Between Heaven and Hell* (InterVarsity Press, 1982) pp. 31-32.
2. A. J. Hoover, *Don't You Believe It* (Moody Press, 1975) p. 122.
3. Stephen C. Meyer, "A Scopes Trial for the '90s," *The Wall Street Journal* (Dec. 6, 1993).
4. *Noah Webster's First Edition of an American Dictionary of the English Language,* republished from 1828 edition with permission from G. & C. Merriam Company by Foundation for American Christian Education, San Francisco, 1980.

Chapter 6

1. *The New Encyclopedia Britannica,* Vol. 8, p. 172.
2. David Barton, *What Happened in Education* (WallBuilders Press, 1990) p. 35. Other books by David Barton (all available from WallBuilder Press, P.O. Box 397, Aledo, TX 76008) include: *The Myth of Separation, America: To Pray or Not To Pray, The Bulletproof George Washington, What Happened in Education?, Did Television Cause the Changes in Youth Morality?, Advice to the Young* and *The New England Primer.*
3. *Christianity Today* (Sept. 13, 1993) pp. 52-54.
4. David Gyertson, ed., *Salt and Light* (Word, 1993) p. 202.
5. Charles Colson and Jack Eckerd, *Why America Doesn't Work* (Word, 1991) p. 68.

Chapter 8

1. *Charisma & Christian Life* (Sept. 1993) p. 36.
2. Ibid, p. 33.
3. Contact The American Center for Law and Justice in Atlanta at 804/523-7546 (phone) or 804/523-7570 (fax).
4. *Charisma & Christian Life* (Sept. 1993) p. 36.
5. Ibid., pp. 33-34.
6. "Without A Prayer," *Time* (Dec. 20, 1993) p. 41.

Chapter 9

1. David Gyertson, ed., *Salt and Light* (Word, 1993) p. 245.
2. *National & International Religion Report* (Nov. 1, 1993) p. 2.
3. Herbert Schlossberg, *Idols For Destruction* (Crossway, 1990) p. xiii.
4. *True Love Waits—A Fact Sheet* (Baptist Sunday School Board, Dec. 1993).
5. MacBeth, Act V, Scene 1.

Chapter 10

1. Sydney E. Alstrom, *A Religious History of the American People,* Vol. 1 (Image Books) pp. 579-80,
2. Paul Thigpen, "The Second Coming: How Many Views," *Charisma & Christian Life* (Feb. 1989) p. 42.
3. *Time* (April 5, 1993) pp. 46-47.
4. *Charisma & Christian Life* (Dec. 1991) pp. 35-36.

THE CARMAN DISCOGRAPHY
Available from Sparrow

Radically Saved
"I've Been Delivered"
"Lord of All"
"Radically Saved"
"No Way, We Are Not Ashamed"
"Soap Song"
"Celebrating Jesus"
"Bless God"
"Jericho: The Shout of Victory"
"I Feel Jesus"
"God of All Nations Medley"
Available on cassette and compact disc

Revival In The Land
"God's Got an Army"
"I Got the Joy"
"A Witch's Invitation"
"Get Your Business Straight with God"
"This Blood"
"Saved, Delivered and Healed"
"Jesus Is the Light"
"The Resurrection Rap"
"Shine Through Me"
"Revival in the Land"
Available on cassette and compact disc

Addicted To Jesus
"Our Turn Now"
"Holy Ghost Hop"
"Satan, Bite the Dust!"
"1955"
"Hunger for Holiness"
"Come into this House"
"Addicted to Jesus"
"Jesus Is the Way"
"The Third Heaven"
Available on cassette and compact disc

Addicted To Jesus video
"Come into this House"
"1955"
"Our Turn Now"
"Satan Bite the Dust"
"Hunger for Holiness"
"Addicted to Jesus"
"Holy Ghost Hop"

The Absolute Best
"I Got the Joy"
"Sunday's on the Way"
"Revive Us, Oh Lord"
"Lazarus Come Forth"
"Soap Song"
"Lord of All"
"Revival in the Land"
"God's Got an Army"
"No Way, We Are Not Ashamed"
"Radically Saved"
"This Blood"
"Fear Not My Child"
"Celebrating Jesus"
"The Champion"
"Serve the Lord"
Available on cassette and compact disc

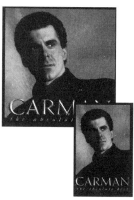

The Standard
"Who's in the House"
"Now's the Time"
"Great God"
"Everybody Praise the Lord"
"The River"
"Marchin' and Movin'"
"Sunday School Rock"
"Holdin' On"
"Lord, I Love You"
"America Again"
Available on cassette and compact disc

The Standard video
"Who's in the House"
"America Again"
"Great God"
"Serve the Lord"
"Holdin' On"
"Sunday School Rock"

To a crowd of over 50,000 people at his "Music for Peace" concert in Johannesburg, Carman presents the "Prince of Peace" to South Africans

*During his concerts,
Carman shares
not only in song,
but from the
Word of God.*

Carman on the set of Time 2 Club Video.

*A scene from
Carman's song, "Great God,"
from The Standard video*

Carman ministering at Beach Reach '93 in Daytona Beach, Florida during spring break.

IT'S <u>TIME</u> 2 JOIN CARMAN'S HOT NEW VIDEO CLUB!

GREAT MUSIC In an age where music and television are distracting and diluting the minds of our young people, it's *TIME 2* pray, *TIME 2* learn and *TIME 2* make a difference in our world for Jesus. *TIME 2*, hosted by Carman, is a high-energy video series that deals with the hardhitting issues that face our youth and world today.

Each thirty-minute video contains live interviews, on-location reports, and today's hottest Christian artists and music videos. Most importantly, each program focuses on Biblical answers to today's toughest questions – from peer pressures and premarital sex to racism and forgiveness – all in a manner that is fun and exciting for pre-teens to parents.

LIVE INTERVIEWS

POWERFUL TOPICS In addition to your family viewing, these outstanding, spiritually inspiring programs can be used as teaching and instructional tools for youth groups and adults, and now the series is available to first-time Video Club members through this special introductory offer.

RECEIVE YOUR FIRST VIDEO FREE!

Order today and receive your first video on Drug Abuse FREE! You will receive each additional video (one per month) at the regular Club price of $19.95 plus shipping and handling and your applicable sales tax.

TO ORDER, CALL 1-800-79TIME2

Other videos in the TIME 2 series:

SINGLE PARENT FAMILIES	**PEER PRESSURE**	**RACISM**
FAITH WITH REASON	**LAST DAYS**	**FORGIVENESS**
TRUTH OR CONSEQUENCES, PT. 1	**NEW AGE**	**EVANGELISM**
TRUTH OR CONSEQUENCES, PT. 2	**HEAVEN**	**PSYCHICS**

30CBA

Distributed by Family Entertainment, A Nest Entertainment Company

To let others know you are

RAISING THE STANDARD

in your world,
order and wear these items
(all feature the Christian Flag as a theme).

RAISING THE STANDARD Product

White Shirt
     Short Sleeve ....($20)
     Long Sleeve ....($25)
     Sweatshirt...............................($30)
Cap...($25)
Silver Key Chain .... ($5)
Gold Key Chain .... ($5)
Choker Necklace.......................... ($5)
Dog Tag .... ($4)

For information on how to order, contact:

PRODUCT DEPARTMENT
c/o Carman Ministries
P.O. Box 701050, Tulsa OK 74170
918/250-1529   Fax 918/251-4492

About Carman Ministries

M I N I S T R I E S

Our objective here at Carman Ministries is to minister to the Body of Christ and to see lost souls won to the Lord. All of our concerts are done on a free admission - love offering basis. Also, I personally write a monthly newsletter that goes out to all of our financial supporters. If you wish to be on the Carman Ministries mailing list and be notified of upcoming concerts in your area, or become a supporter and receive our monthly newsletter, write:

Carman Ministries
P.O. Box 701050
Tulsa, Oklahoma 74170

(918) 250-1529
Fax (918) 251-4492

Join us in winning this generation
for Jesus Christ!

Let's Put God In America Again!

I am writing to you not only as a fellow believer, but as an American concerned about the standard of life in our country. The headlines of our local newspapers tell us stories that are of nightmarish proportions. Things are happening in our nation that were unimaginable in the 40's and 50's, all because of an event which took place in 1962 that changed the course of American history forever.

This was when the Supreme Court ruled that prayer was to be abolished from the United States classroom. This decision was monumental in that it was the first time in the history of our nation, three hundred and forty-two years since the pilgrims and one hundred and seventy-three years since the Constitution, that America took a verbal public stance against God. Abraham Lincoln said, "*The philosophy of the schoolroom in one generation will be the philosophy of the government in the next.*"

When the Body of Christ allowed people to speak out against God in 1962, our nation began an unprecedented rise in immorality, since then…

Divorce has increased 117%
Adultery has increased 200%
Sexually transmitted diseases among ages 15-20, up 226%
Teenage suicide up 253%
Unwed mother birthrate, ages 10-14, up 553%
Unmarried couples living together increased by 536%
Violent crime up 794% and
Sexual abuse of children is up a horrifying 2,000%*

Now, these are just eight of the forty categories reflecting the increase in national immorality. John Adams, our second President, stated, "*Our Constitution was written only for a religious and moral people. It will not work to govern any other people.*" If we do not take a stand for righteousness now, this country will continue to self-destruct. The Word of God emphatically states in Proverbs 14:34 that **"Righteousness exalteth a nation, but sin is a reproach to any people."**

So what can we do now? I believe that it's time to sound the alarm from the church house to the White House and say we need God in America again! God has laid it upon my heart to gather at least 1 million signatures on a petition from people of all ages who support a Constitutional Amendment that would allow voluntary prayer back into our public schools systems.

Through music God has given me the eyes and the ears of an entire generation, and I want to use that influence for His glory. Now as the people of God, I need your help by signing the enclosed petition card indicating your support for this amendment.

By uniting together, we will make a tremendous difference for the Lord Jesus Christ and America can once again be a safe place to raise our children. For the Scriptures promise us in *Psalm 33:12*, "Blessed is the nation whose God is the Lord." I am asking you, as salt and light in this wounded and dying nation, to help us rebuild the fallen walls of our country and put God in America Again.

* *All sources and figures gathered from David Barton and Wall Builders Press.*

Let's Put God In America Again!

Carman, I join you in supporting a Constitutional Amendment permitting voluntary prayer in the Public School Systems.

(Please copy and give to a friend! Only 1 person per card. Please print clearly.)

Name _____

Date of Birth _____ /_____ /_____ ❑ Male ❑ Female
               MO.   DAY   YEAR

Address_____

City _____ State _____ Zip_____

Daytime Phone (   ) _____

Evening Phone (   ) _____

Signature _____

Date_____

❑ Please send me more information on Carman Ministries.

❑ Please use my name and address for this petition only.

Complete and mail to:

AMERICA AGAIN
c/o Carman Ministries
P.O. Box 701050
Tulsa, OK 74170

Phone (918) 250-1529   Fax (918) 251-4492